The VERY NICE
JEWISH QUIZ BOOK

THE
VERY NICE
JEWISH QUIZ BOOK

Dan Carlinsky

BELL PUBLISHING COMPANY
New York

This 1987 edition is published by Bell Publishing
Company, distributed by Crown Publishers, Inc.,
225 Park Avenue South, New York, New York 10003,
by arrangement with Carlinsky and Carlinsky, Inc.

Printed and bound in the United States of America

Library of Congress Cataloging-in-Publication Data
Carlinsky, Dan.
The very nice Jewish quiz book.
Rev. ed. of: The Jewish quiz book. 1979.
1. Jews—Miscellanea.   I. Carlinsky, Dan.   Jewish
quiz book.   II. Title.
DS118.5.C37   1987   909'.04924   87-12432
ISBN 0-517-64294-8

h g f e d c b a

CONTENTS

vi

—— WHAT'S IT ALL ABOUT? ——

This is not a serious book about the Jewish religion. Nor about Jewish culture or history. This is simply a fun book for anyone who eats bagels and cream cheese on Sunday mornings.

It's a quiz book about who's Jewish and what's Jewish, Jewish singers and Jewish boxers, Jewish quotes and Jewish jokes, Israeli geography and Yiddish curses, chopped liver and the Marx Brothers. In a phrase, Jewish pop. Plenty of it.

Add some tests and puzzles on Jewish holidays and the Bible, on rabbis and prayers, and you have more than eleven hundred questions and answers on things Jewish.

The quizzes are meant to make you kvell (when you know the answer), to tantalize you (when you don't but are sure you once did), to instruct you (when you look it up).

There's no scoring system. The best way to judge your performance is to read the questions to someone else. Whoever says, "Aha! You don't know that?" most often is the winner.

Read it in good health.

Dan Carlinsky

The VERY NICE
JEWISH QUIZ BOOK

—— BY ANY OTHER NAME ——

Jews who accomplish something, who stand out in the crowd, often pick up a title or nickname along the way. Here's a list of such. Behind each entry is a famous Jew—past or present, arts or letters, sports or show business . . . or another field. How many do you know?

1. "The King of Swing"
2. "The Giant Killer"
3. "The Toastmaster General of the United States"
4. "The Last of the Red-Hot Mamas"
5. "The Voice of the New York Yankees"
6. "Slapsie Maxie"
7. "Hammerin' Hank"
8. "The Great Jewish Buddha"
9. "The Vamp"
10. "The Lady in Mink"
11. "The Divine Miss M"
12. "The Henry Ford of France"
13. "Adviser to Presidents"
14. "Mr. Television"
15. "Minnie's Boys"
16. "Henry the K"
17. "Murray the K"
18. "The Brains of the Confederacy"
19. "Bubbles"
20. "Banjo Eyes"

Answers

1. Jazzman Benny Goodman. 2. David, of slingshot fame. 3. Entertainer George Jessel. 4. Singer Sophie Tucker. 5. Sportscaster Mel Allen (born Melvin Israel). 6. Boxer Maxie Rosenbloom. 7. Home-run hitter Hank Greenberg. 8. Writer Gertrude Stein. 9. The first silent-film siren, Theda Bara (born Theodosia Goodman). 10. Bess Myerson, on TV's "The Big Payoff." 11. Singer Bette Midler. 12. Auto maker André-Gustave Citroën. 13. Financier Bernard Baruch. 14. Comedian Milton Berle (born Berlinger). 15. The Marx Brothers. 16. Secretary of State Henry Kissinger. 17. Disk jockey Murray Kaufman, also known as "the fifth Beatle." 18. Confederate statesman Judah P. Benjamin. 19. Opera star Beverly Sills. 20. Entertainer Eddie Cantor.

—— AN UNCOMMON QUIZ ——

Fifteen small groups—and your job is to tell what the members of each group have in common. Can you do it?

1. Marilyn Monroe, Elizabeth Taylor, and Sammy Davis, Jr.
2. Dr. Hugo Z. Hackenbush, Rufus T. Firefly, and Otis B. Driftwood.
3. Léon Blum, Benjamin Disraeli, Alfred Isaac Isaacs, Bruno Kreisky, and Luigi Luzzatti.
4. Wilhelm Steinitz and Emanuel Lasker.
5. Tishman, Uris, and Rudin.
6. The sexton in a synagogue and the ninth candle on a Chanukah menorah.
7. Father Coughlin and Gerald L. K. Smith.
8. Alicia Markova and Anna Pavlova (besides their rhyming names).
9. Kurt Baum and Richard Tucker.
10. Schapiro, Kedem, Duc de Provence, Monarch, and Carmel.
11. Morton Schwartz, Max Hirsch, and Ira Hanford.
12. Beet soup and the Catskill Mountains.

2

13. "What is hateful to thee, do not unto thy fellow man" and "Look not at the flask but at what it contains."
14. The destruction of the First Temple at Jerusalem, the destruction of the Second Temple, and the expulsion of the Jews from Spain.
15. Treblinka and Belzec.

Answers

1. All converted to Judaism. 2. All are characters played in films by Groucho Marx: Hackenbush in *A Day at the Races*, Firefly in *Duck Soup*, Driftwood in *A Night at the Opera*. 3. Each was a head of government and each was Jewish-born: Blum was premier of France; Disraeli, prime minister of Britain; Isaacs, governor-general of Australia; Kreisky, premier of Austria; Luzzatti, prime minister of Italy. 4. Each held the world chess championship for more than a quarter century. 5. All are important New York builders. 6. Both are called shammes. 7. Both were loud anti-Jewish demagogues. 8. Both were ballerinas. 9. Both were Jewish tenors who sang at the Metropolitan Opera. 10. All make kosher wines. 11. They were owner, trainer, and jockey of Bold Venture, the 1936 Kentucky Derby winner. (All but the horse were Jewish.) 12. Beet soup is borscht and the Catskills are the home of Jewish resort hotels, "the Borscht Belt." 13. Both quotes are from the Talmud. 14. All are traditionally held to have occurred on the ninth of Av, Tisha b'Av. 15. Both were World War II extermination camps in Poland.

—— JEWISH FOOD ——

The big problem with eating a full meal of Jewish food, so the saying goes, is that three days later you're hungry again. Even reading about Jewish food tastes good. So taste.

For starters, prove you're in the ball game by matching these two-word food names:

1. Cheese   matzoh
2. Lokshen   fish
3. Kasha   cabbage
4. Chopped   blintzes
5. Egg   liver
6. Gefilte   kugel
7. Dill   bagel
8. Onion   pickle
9. Gedempte   varnishkehs
10. Stuffed   fleysh

11. What does a bagel have that a bialy doesn't?
12. What's known as the Bread of Affliction?
13. What's the difference between stuffed derma and kishkeh?
14. What's helzel?

What best accompanies these foods? Match.

15. gefilte fish   sour cream
16. potato latkes   horseradish
17. blintzes   knaydlach
18. chicken soup   sour cream

19. What's the basic ingredient of the usual tzimmes?
20. Is mandelbroit an appetizer, a meat dish, or a dessert?
21. Would you typically eat matzoh brei for breakfast, for dinner, or as a snack?
22. How about kasha? Is it usually eaten for breakfast, as a side dish, or as a snack?

4

23. What's wrong with the concept of instant cholent?
24. What's mohn?
25. Which wouldn't you use to fill a knish: potato, kasha, meat, or honey?
26. Which generally costs more, lox or nova?
27. What's "for two cents plain"?
28. What's the meaning of the little ʊ found on packages of various foods in supermarkets?
29. Take some chicken fat and skin. Cut it into small pieces. Heat with chopped onions in a pan. When skin is crisp and onions are brown, cool and strain. What have you got?
30. What's the Jewish equivalent of ravioli or won ton?

Answers

1. Cheese blintzes. 2. Lokshen kugel. 3. Kasha varnishkehs. 4. Chopped liver. 5. Egg matzoh. 6. Gefilte fish. 7. Dill pickle. 8. Onion bagel. 9. Gedempte fleysh. 10. Stuffed cabbage. 11. A hole. 12. Matzoh. 13. Nothing; they're two names for the same thing, that being stuffed intestine. 14. Stuffed poultry-neck skins. 15. Horseradish. 16. Sour cream. 17. Sour cream. 18. Knaydlach. 19. Carrots. 20. A dessert (a pastry, to be more precise). 21. For breakfast (unless you *really* love matzoh brei, in which case all three). 22. As a side dish. 23. Cholent is a meat-and-beans stew that was designed to cook overnight . . . *at least;* it came about because of the ban on Sabbath cooking. You could light a fire under a pot of ingredients just before sundown Friday and the next day, presto! Cholent! 24. Poppy seed. 25. Honey would make a lousy knish. 26. Nova. 27. Many years ago it was a large glass of seltzer. (Today, of course, "for two cents plain" costs about a quarter.) 28. It's the "kosher" symbol of the Union of Orthodox Jewish Congregations of America. 29. Gribenes, or greeven. 30. Kreplach.

5

—— WHAT'S KOSHER? ——

Everyone knows the word, but not everyone knows just what is strictly kosher and what must be counted as the opposite: trayf. Mark a "K" or a "T" next to each of these:

1. Grasshoppers _____
2. Squid _____
3. Cornish hen _____
4. Seagull eggs _____
5. Sturgeon _____
6. Deer _____
7. Owl _____
8. Goat _____
9. Zucchini _____
10. Oysters _____
11. Swan _____
12. Camel _____
13. Anchovies _____
14. Smelt _____
15. Whale _____
16. Porpoise _____
17. Turtle _____
18. Shredded Wheat _____

19. Why is meat salted and rinsed as part of the koshering process?
20. What's written in the window of kosher butcher shops?

Answers

1. K. 2. T. 3. K. 4. T. 5. T. 6. K. 7. T. 8. K. 9. K. 10. T. 11. T. 12. T. 13. K. 14. K. 15. T. 16. T. 17. T. 18. K. 19. To remove the blood, which is forbidden. 20. Basar kosher—kosher meat.

6

To many, a good part of being Jewish is hearing, appreciating, and repeating Jewish jokes. Here's the first of twelve classics that appear throughout the book. If you've heard them before, good—you'll be asked to supply the missing punch lines.

HAVE YOU HEARD
THIS ONE?

"Hello—Cooperstein, Cooperstein, Cooperstein, and Cooperstein."

"Hello, I'd like to speak with Mr. Cooperstein."

"Mr. Cooperstein is in Chicago today."

"Okay, then let me speak to Mr. Cooperstein."

"Sorry, he'll be in court until this afternoon."

"Well, I'll talk to Mr. Cooperstein, then."

"I'm afraid he's in an important meeting."

"Oh, all right. I'll talk to Mr. Cooperstein."

"————————————————!"

"Speaking!"

—— BRAND NAMES ——

TV advertising notwithstanding, there's more to brand-name Jewish foods than Hebrew National. For instance, match these brands with the product they're best known for:

1. Horowitz Margareten   frozen chicken
2. Barton   margarine
3. Empire   frozen bagels
4. Lender   matzoh
5. Mother's   chocolate

6. Streit and Goodman are two other manufacturers of one of the five products above. Which?
7. Fox's U-Bet is a favorite mixer. Exactly what is it?
8. Rokeach makes, among many other things, a product that comes in two varieties: with the word "kosher" marked in red and with the word in blue. What is it?
9. Which flavor *doesn't* Manischewitz make?
   A. Blackberry   C. Cherry
   B. Strawberry   D. Elderberry
          E. Loganberry
10. What's the Jewish product that sponsored Jan Murray's "Dollar a Second" television show in the fifties?

Answers

8

—— THE YIDDISH LANGUAGE ——

For millions of Jews, still, it's the mama-loshen—the mother tongue. For tens of millions of Americans, Jewish or not, many of its words have sneaked into the national consciousness by way of show business. Thus, this extensive quiz on the language, in four parts. (Note: Please don't bother the author with quibbles about English spelling of Yiddish words. He has enough tsuris.)

1. If your daughter—not a shayne maydel—turned twenty-five and was still living at home with you, would you send for
    A. the moel?   C. the shochet?
    B. the rebbetzin?   D. the shadchan?
                    E. the chazzan?
2. A friend calls to announce, "I want to tell you about a simcha." What should you expect to hear about?
3. If your son came home with a girl who was descended from a long line of losers with absolutely no status or redeeming features, you might complain (quietly) that she had no what?
4. If you tell someone you shep naches from your child, are you bragging or complaining?
5. If you're the superstitious type, you'll know the right Yiddish phrase to round out this sentence: "Ah, Mrs. Goldblatt, you're looking very well, _____ _____."
6. And you might know how to complete this: "Yes, I always liked your grandfather, _____ _____."
7. Where would you hope to find a first-rate tummler?
    A. in a deli   C. in a Borscht Belt hotel
    B. in a dairy restaurant D. in the ocean
                    E. in shul
8. A person who kills his mother and father and then pleads with the court for mercy because he's an orphan is demonstrating the classic example of _____.
9. What's the masculine form of the word shikseh?

9

10. What's the name for the little box in which change is collected for charity?

11. Speaking of which, what's the word for charity?

12. On your way into shul you notice a diamond ring on the sidewalk. Since it's shabbes, you don't pick it up, of course, but you deftly kick it behind a bush and return after sundown. Monday morning, bright and early, you rush to a jeweler. He peers through his glass and says, "I must tell you this ring is really worth bubkis." Is it a lucky find or not?

13. Which of the following are zoftig?
    A. Phyllis Diller   C. Elizabeth Taylor
    B. Shelley Winters   D. Beatrice Arthur

14. William Shakespeare—who *wasn't* Jewish—called one of his plays *Much Ado About Nothing.* Had the Bard known a little Yiddish, he could have reduced that title to just one delicious word, which is also the name of a tasty dish. What?

15. If that fellow over there is a bissel farblondjet, is he
    A. a sour Scandinavian? C. a little mixed up?
    B. a tiny spicy meatball? D. a Hungarian carpet sweeper?

16. If I need something vi a loch in kop, how badly do I need it?

17. Are a k'nocker and a nebbech similar or different?

18. If you want to start a discussion, you can point out that Adam had no shviger and no pupik. Meaning . . . ?

19. You are a fashionable woman. You are dressed in your latest outfit—very smashing, if you do say so yourself. You go to your mah-jongg club and as you approach two women, you hear one whisper, "Here she comes—doesn't she look like a real kurveh in that outfit?" Should you smile and thank her or pour tea on her dress?

20. You are a tired woman. You have been shlepping yourself around from early morning, running here and there, buying this and that, carrying bundles and packages. Finally you reach home, thoroughly—but *thoroughly*—exhausted. You drop your things on the bed and before you even make yourself a nice glass of hot tea with lemon you do what you've been dying to do all day long: you take off your girdle. One

word, and one word only, will do for the feeling you get. "Oy!" you sigh, "is this a _____!"

Answers

1. *D*, the shadchan (matchmaker). (The others are: A. the circumciser, B. the rabbi's wife, C. the ritual butcher, E. the cantor.). 2. A happy occasion. 3. No yichus (family background, pedigree). 4. You're bragging—it means you're basking in pride over him. 5. Kayn ainhoreh (meaning there should be "no evil eye"). 6. Alav hashalom ("May he rest in peace."). 7. C. In a Borscht Belt hotel, because a tummler is a live-wire emcee. 8. Chutzpah. 9. Shaygetz. 10. Pushkeh. 11. Tzedakah. 12. Not—it's worthless. 13. All but A. would qualify—they have those few extra cuddly pounds. 14. Tzimmes. 15. C. a little mixed up. 16. Not at all—in fact, "like a hole in the head." 17. Very different—the first is a big shot, the second a little nothing. 18. No mother-in-law and no navel. 19. Start pouring—a kurveh is a prostitute. 20. Mechaieh.

HAVE YOU HEARD THIS ONE?

Abramowitz and his wife went to Rome. When he returned, Abramowitz's pals in the Garment District asked all about his trip. "We went to the Vatican," Abramowitz beamed, "and had an audience with the Pope himself!"
"The Pope! What does he look like?"
"_____"

"About a 42 long."

YIDDISH: THE "SHHH!" FACTOR

There is no shortage of the "sh" sound in Yiddish. Here are twenty of them, in definition form. You match the right words. Score sixteen right and you're a shayner Yid; less than ten and you're something of a shmo; less than five and you're a real shmegeggi.

1. Pipsqueak/fool	Shikker
2. Detective	Shlep
3. Little town	Shmaltz
4. Wig	Shmendrik
5. Match (the marriage kind)	Shtetl
6. Drunk	Shtik
7. Carry or drag	Shul
8. Chintzy	Shnorrer
9. Sentimental corn	Shlock
10. Rag	Shmooz
11. Chat and gossip	Shaytl
12. Whiskey or brandy	Shammes
13. Nose	Shnoz
14. Piece or actor's little routine	Shtarker
15. Synagogue	Shmatteh
16. Beautiful	Shiddach
17. Scandal	Shnapps
18. Strong or brave one	Shvitz
19. Sweat	Shandeh
20. Professional beggar	Shayn

Answers

1. Shmendrik. 2. Shammes. 3. Shtetl. 4. Shaytl. 5. Shiddach. 6. Shikker. 7. Shlep. 8. Shlock. 9. Shmaltz. 10. Shmatteh. 11. Shmooz. 12. Shnapps. 13. Shnoz. 14. Shtik. 15. Shul. 16. Shayn. 17. Shandeh. 18. Shtarker. 19. Shvitz. 20. Shnorrer.

YIDDISH:
—— WHAT'S THE DIFFERENCE? ——

Do you know the difference between . . .

1. . . . a shlemiel and a shlimazel?
2. . . . a mensch and a meshuggener?
3. . . . a chassen and a chazzan?
4. . . . a kalleh and a kallikeh?
5. . . . saychel and meichel?
6. . . . kvetch and kvell?
7. . . . a Moishe Kapoyr and a Kuni Lemmel?
8. . . . a shvoger and a shvegerin?
9. . . . essen and fressen?
10. . . . your punim and your pupik?

Answers

1. A shlemiel's bad luck is brought on by his own clumsy actions; a shlimazel's troubles come about through no action of his own, but just because he's a shlimazel. A shlemiel of a waiter, for instance, trips and spills the hot soup. On whom does he spill it? The shlimazel. 2. A mensch is a fine human being, a meshuggener a crazy man. 3. A chassen is a bridegroom, a chazzan a cantor. 4. A kalleh is a bride, a kallikeh a cripple. 5. Saychel is common sense, a meichel is a delicacy. 6. To kvetch is to complain—over and over; to kvell is to puff out the chest and take pride. 7. A Moishe Kapoyr is an ornery, contradictory person, a Kuni Lemmel a Simple Simon. 8. A shvoger is a brother-in-law, a shvegerin a sister-in-law. 9. Essen is to eat (which you should), Fressen is to gobble like an animal (which you shouldn't). 10. Plenty, one hopes: your punim is your face, your pupik your navel.

13

YIDDISH:
── COMPLETE THE EXPRESSIONS ──

The first is a complaint, the second a curse, the third a vulgar phrase, the fourth a nasty order, and only the fifth is something nice to say. Can you finish them and interpret?

1. "A klog tzu . . ."   3. "A potch in . . ."
2. "Gay feifen af'n . . ."   4. "Hok nit kayn . . ."
                  5. "Trog . . ."

Answers

1. ". . . Columbus'n." ("A curse on Columbus," meaning, approximately, "If he hadn't gone and found America I wouldn't be in this fix.") 2. ". . . yam." ("Go whistle on the ocean.") 3. ". . . tuchis." (A potch in tuchis is a slap where you sit down.) 4. ". . . tchainik." ("Don't go on and on so"; literally, "Don't beat on a kettle.") 5. ". . . gezunterhayt." ("Wear it in good health.")

── REMEMBER HEBREW SCHOOL? ──

No? Well, here's a Hebrew test for people who don't really know Hebrew. Most of the questions deal with the kind of knowledge that's picked up outside the Hebrew classroom. Try them.

1. Jews frequently say "Mazel tov!" when they mean "Congratulations!" Literally, however, the phrase means . . . ?
2. What's the usual response to "Shalom aleichem!"
3. What's the difference between "L'chaim!" (the universal Jewish toast) and "À votre santé!" (the French "Cheers!")?

14

4. Rosh Hashonah, you know, is the Jewish New Year. But what do the words mean literally?
5. The Seder is the Passover ritual meal. What does that word mean?
6. In prayer, God's name is Adonai. What substitute name is used in rehearsing prayers, to avoid pronouncing the divine name?
7. What Hebrew word refers to both a synagogue activity and a certain type of voyage?
8. Israel's national anthem is "Hatikvah," meaning . . . ?
9. Surely you know of El Al, Israel's national airline. But what does that name signify?
10. With what do you associate the Hebrew phrase mah nishtana?

Answers

1. "Good luck!" 2. "Aleichem shalom!" 3. The French drink to each other's health, the Jews "to life." 4. Head of the year. 5. Order, or ceremony. 6. Adoshem. 7. Aliyah (literally, going up), which means being called to read the Torah as well as migration to Israel. 8. "The Hope." 9. Upward, or up in the air. 10. The Passover Seder; it's the first two words of the Four Questions.

—— IT'S LIKE THIS ——

Yiddish and Hebrew combine to make up this little game, in which you're asked to pick the word that's closest in meaning to the italicized word at the left. Just circle your answers.

1. *Dayenu*   avek   af'n tish   genug
2. *Balabuste*   shvitzer   beryeh   nosher
3. *Mazuma*   gelt   vasser   meeskeit
4. *Mechuleh*   meshuggeh   kaput   af shpilkehs
5. *Sheket!*   shalom!   shah!   ·   todah!

Answers

1. Genug: enough, sufficient. 2. Beryeh: a great homemaker. 3. Gelt: cash. 4. Kaput: through, finished. 5. Shah!: quiet!

—— MAKE THE ASSOCIATIONS ——

Everything and everybody on the left is normally associated with something or somebody on the right. Match 'em up.

1. Gragger   nursing homes
2. Samuel Bronfman   Sophie Tucker
3. Etrog   Chanukah
4. "My Man"   knish
5. "Some of These Days" Passover
6. Isaac Mayer Wise   Fanny Brice
7. "Maoz Tzur"   Seagram's whiskey
8. Yonah Shimmel   Haman
9. Bernard Bergman   lulav
10. "Dayenu"   Reform Judaism

16

HAVE YOU HEARD THIS ONE?

 A mother gives her son Mendl not one but *two* neckties for Chanukah. Being a clever and loving son, Mendl makes sure to wear one of the ties the very next time he visits for Friday-night dinner. His Jewish mama takes one look and says, "_____ _____?"

"Vot's de madder? De odder vun you don't like?"

17

—— JEWISH ANALOGIES ——

The form is classic college board: the first is to the second as the third is to the fourth. Relationships vary from example to example. Fill in the missing entries.

1. Rabbi:rebbetzin:: _____:bobbeh.
2. Get:ketubah::averah: _____.
3. Megilah:Purim::_____:Pesach.
4. Ashkenazim:Yiddish::Sephardim: _____.
5. A.D.:C.E.::B.C.: _____.

Answers

1. **Zaydeh.** (The rabbi is married to the rabbi's wife; the grandfather is married to the grandmother.) 2. **Mitzvah.** (A divorce decree is the opposite of a marriage contract; a sin is the opposite of a good deed.) 3. **Haggadah.** (The Megilla is the book that tells the story of Purim; the Haggadah is the book that tells of Passover.) 4. **Ladino.** (Central and Eastern European Jews speak Yiddish; Spanish and Portuguese Jews speak Ladino.) 5. **B.C.E.** (Anno Domini is, by Hebrew reckoning, the Common Era; Before Christ is Before the Common Era.)

—— MATCHING EXPRESSIONS ——

Here are ten 2-word expressions having one thing or another to do with Jewishness. Only trouble is, they're split up and jumbled around into two columns. Start with the left-hand word and find a word on the right to complete the expression.

1. Chanukah	calf
2. Yortzeit	mitzvah
3. Oneg	goy
4. Golden	cap
5. Eternal	bond
6. Brit	candle
7. Skull	light
8. Israel	milah
9. Shabbes	gelt
10. Bat	Shabbat

Answers

1. Chanukah gelt. 2. Yortzeit candle. 3. Oneg Shabbat. 4. Golden calf. 5. Eternal light. 6. Brit milah. 7. Skullcap. 8. Israel bond. 9. Shabbes goy. 10. Bat Mitzvah.

—— WHAT'S THE DIFFERENCE . . . ? ——

1. . . . between kiddush and kaddish?
2. . . . between a seder and a siddur?
3. . . . between Golan and golem?
4. . . . between a yeshiva and a cheder?
5. . . . between a yarmulkeh and a kipah?

Answers

1. Kiddush is a sabbath and holiday prayer; kaddish is generally a mourner's prayer. 2. A seder is the Passover meal; a siddur is a prayer book. 3. Golan is an area east of the Jordan River; a golem, according to legend, is a humanlike supernatural creation—sort of a Jewish Frankenstein's monster. 4. A yeshiva is a school for religious and secular studies; a cheder is for basic Hebrew language only. 5. No difference—the first is Yiddish, the second is Hebrew; both mean skullcap.

—— THE JEWISH-MOTHER PUZZLE ——

Five questions about the greatest cliché of them all. Fill in the squares with the answers.

1. What's Alex Portnoy's Jewish Mother's first name?
2. Jewish Mother's dinner-table refrain: "Ess, ess, _____
_____."
3. Miss Tucker's song: "My _____ _____."
4. Where did Georgie Jessel find a bright and guiding light?
5. Mrs. Berle, the classic stage mama—what was her first name?

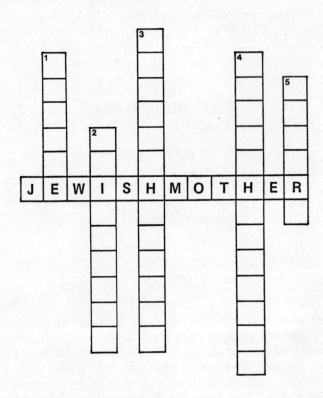

Answers

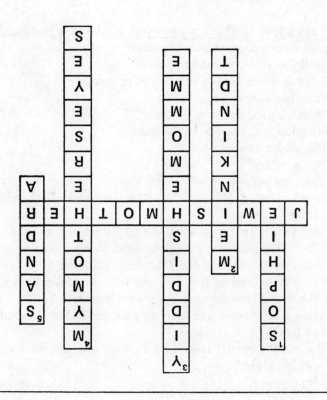

___ ...AND I QUOTE... ___

A mixed bag of good lines from quotable, notable Jews throughout history. Who said . . . ?

1. "I am a Jew. Hath not a Jew eyes? Hath not a Jew hands, organs, dimensions, senses, affections, passions?"
2. "Will you still love me tomorrow?"
3. "Love is never having to say you're sorry."
4. "Rose is a rose is a rose."
5. "Who's buried in Grant's Tomb?"
6. "Religion is the opiate of the masses."
7. "Ida, sweet as apple cider."
8. "Never mind!"
9. "Take my wife—please!"
10. "Good evening, Mr. and Mrs. America and all the ships at sea: let's go to press!"
11. "Yes, I am a Jew, and when the ancestors of the right honorable gentleman were brutal savages living in caves, my ancestors were priests in the Temple of Solomon."
12. "What is hateful to thee, do not unto thy fellow man. This is the whole law; the rest is mere commentary."
13. "More than Israel has kept the Sabbath, the Sabbath has kept Israel."
14. "Bisexuality immediately doubles your chances for a date on Saturday night."
15. "Mmmmm*wa!*"

Answers

1. Shylock, in Shakespeare's *The Merchant of Venice*. 2. Carole King, on the *Tapestries* album. 3. Erich Segal, in *Love Story*. 4. Gertrude Stein, in *Sacred Emily*. 5. Groucho Marx, on his "You Bet Your Life" TV quiz show. 6. Karl Marx. 7. Eddie Cantor. 8. Gilda Radner, as Emily Litella on TV's "Saturday Night." 9. Henny Youngman. 10. Walter Winchell. 11. Disraeli. 12. Hillel. 13. Ahad Ha-am. 14. Woody Allen. 15. Dinah (born Frances Rose) Shore, throwing her trademark kiss.

HAVE YOU HEARD
THIS ONE?

FIRST CUSTOMER: "Waiter! Tea—in a glass."
SECOND CUSTOMER: "Also tea for me . . . and make sure the glass is clean!"

(Waiter exits, then returns with tray.)
WAITER: "_____?"

"All right, two teas. Now, who wanted the clean glass?"

23

—— COMPLETE THE QUOTE ——

These brief, well-known quotes and expressions range from a centuries-old wish to a modern advertising slogan—from the sublime to the ridiculous, you might say. Finish them.

1. "Let my people . . ."
2. "You don't have to be Jewish . . ."
3. "Leshanah tova . . ."
4. "Next year . . ."
5. "Sheila Levine Is . . ."
6. "Man, oh Manischewitz . . ."
7. "Hava . . ."
8. "Eretz . . ."
9. "As long as you have your . . ."
10. "Thy people shall be my people and thy God my God."
    What lines come just *before* that?

Answers

1. ". . . go!" (Attributed by song to Moses, adopted by defenders of Soviet Jewry)   2. ". . . to love Levy's." (Ad slogan for a brand of bread)   3. ". . . tikatevu." (The Jewish New Year greeting: "May you be inscribed and sealed for a good year!")   4. ". . . in Jerusalem!" (The annual Passover wish)   5. ". . . Dead and Living in New York." (Book title)   6. ". . . what a wine!" (Ad slogan)   7. ". . . Negila." (Song title)   8. ". . . Yisrael." ("Land of Israel.")   9. ". . . health." (Bit of Jewish wisdom)   10. "Whither thou goest I will go; and where thou lodgest I will lodge." (Said by Ruth to Naomi in the Bible)

— ODD ONE OUT —

Here are ten little lists, ranging from three to six entries each. In each grouping, one member is out of place. Find it.

1. Which of the following is *not*, in Jewish traditions, associated with death?
   A. Uncovering the head C. Tearing clothes
   B. Covering mirrors   D. Sitting on low stools
                E. Eating hard-boiled eggs

2. Which holiday is out of place here?
   A. Yom Kippur   B. Purim
                C. Simchat Torah

3. Edna Ferber was a Jewish Midwesterner who started her career as a teen-aged newspaper reporter. She went on to write important novels, plays, and films. Pick the title she *didn't* write.
   A. *Giant*   C. *Cimarron*
   B. *Show Boat*   D. *So Big*
                E. *The Best of Everything*

4. You've just come in from a cold, rainy outdoors. You sit down to a bowl of piping-hot chicken soup, and is it delicious! Which of these fine Yiddish expressions would you *not* give forth?
   A. "Geshmak!"   C. "Feh!"
   B. "A meichell"   D. "A shaynem dank!"

5. Which quote is *not* from the Bible?
   A. "Vanity of vanities . . . all is vanity."
   B. "There is no new thing under the sun."
   C. "To every thing there is a season, and a time to every purpose under heaven."
   D. "To eat, and to drink, and to be merry."
   E. "We are such stuff as dreams are made on, and our little life is rounded with a sleep."

6. Which word *doesn't* belong in this group?
    A. Siddur   C. Chumash
    B. Haggadah   D. Mikveh
            E. Gemara
7. "Sabra" means three things. Which *doesn't* it mean?
    A. A native-born Israeli
    B. A traditional game
    C. A cactus fruit
    D. An orange-chocolate liqueur
8. Who *doesn't* belong on this list of prominent Jews? Why?
    A. Benjamin Cardozo   D. Arthur Goldberg
    B. Bernard Baruch   E. Felix Frankfurter
    C. Abe Fortas   F. Louis Brandeis
9. Another list of six notable Jewish men. Which is in the wrong company? Why?
    A. Mischa Elman   D. Emil Gilels
    B. Nathan Milstein   E. David Oistrakh
    C. Fritz Kreisler   F. Yehudi Menuhin
10. Which Yiddish expression *isn't* used as a farewell?
    A. "Shalom!"   C. "Gevalt!"
    B. "Zei gezunt!"   D. "A guten tog!"

Answers

1. *A.* Uncovering the head is not a Jewish practice.   2. *A.* Yom Kippur is a sad day; the others are jolly.   3. *E. The Best of Everything* was written by Rona Jaffe.   4. *C.* "Feh!" means "Phooey!" The others mean, in order, "Tasty!," "A delicacy!" and "Thanks a million!"   5. *E.* isn't biblical. It's from Shakespeare's *The Tempest.*   6. *D.* is a ritual bathhouse; the others are all things to be read.   7. *B.* A traditional game it isn't.   8. *B.* Bernard Baruch is the only one who didn't serve on the U. S. Supreme Court.   9. *D.* Emil Gilels is a pianist; the others play—or played—violin.   10. *C.* "Gevalt!" means "Help!" or "Oy!" The others mean, in order, "Peace!," "Be healthy!" and "A good day!"

26

—— IDENTIFICATIONS, PLEASE ——

A this-and-that of people and things, and you are asked to identify. The first ten need matching; in the second batch you're on your own.

1. Henrietta Szold	A. the "Save-Nixon" rabbi
2. Ushpitzin	B. custom of calling a bridegroom to the Torah before his wedding
3. Oswiecim	C. Polish name for Auschwitz
4. Aufruf	D. mystical interpretation of the Bible
5. Kabbalah	
6. Elaine Kaufman	E. one who holds child during circumcision
7. Baruch Korff	
8. Sandek	F. ancient Jewish court
9. Sanhedrin	G. Yiddish name for Auschwitz
10. Irgun Tzevai Leumi	H. owner of a chic Manhattan restaurant
	I. founding president of Hadassah
	J. underground terrorist group led by Menachem Begin during struggle for Israeli independence

11. Black September
12. W. W. Rostow
13. Baal Shem Tov
14. Earl of Beaconsfield
15. Zaddik
16. Drawing of a fist inside a Star of David
17. Pentateuch
18. Kotel Ma'aravi
19. Rambam
20. Shochet

Answers

1. *I.* 2. *G.* 3. *C.* 4. *B.* 5. *D.* 6. *H.* 7. *A.* 8. *E.* 9. *F.* 10. *J.* 11. Arab terrorist group that killed Israeli athlete-hostages at the 1972 Olympics in Munich. 12. One of JFK's "Cambridge Group" advisers, an MIT economist. 13. Founder of Chasidism, in eighteenth-century Lubavitch, Poland. 14. *Title of Benjamin Disraeli.* 15. A righteous, saintly person. 16. *Symbol of the Jewish Defense League.* 17. *The Torah* (the Five Books of Moses): Genesis, Exodus, Leviticus, Numbers, Deuteronomy. 18. The Western Wall. 19. *Name for Moses Maimonides* (from the Hebrew initials of his name, Reb Moses Ben Maimon). 20. Kosher slaughterer.

——— . . . ALSO KNOWN AS . . . ———

Jews of twentieth-century America have often changed their names—particularly when embarking on a career in show business. Three-syllable and four-syllable old-world family names are considered a burden and unlikely to make it to the marquee. Sometimes the name-changing ploy works, sometimes not. Here are some success stories. Guess who.

1. A songwriter named Israel Baline.
2. A songwriter-singer named Robert Zimmerman.
3. A comic named Leonard Hacker.
4. A magician named Ehrich Weiss.
5. A singer named Asa Yoelson.
6. A zany filmmaker named Melvin Kaminsky.
7. A dancer named Arthur M. Teichman.
8. A comedian named Nathan Birnbaum.
9. Another zany filmmaker, named Allen Stewart Konigsberg.
10. An opera singer named Belle Silverman.

And five to match:

11. Louis Schneider   Kirk Douglas
12. Issur Danielovitch Demsky   Edward G. Robinson
13. David Daniel Kaminsky   Lenny Bruce
14. Emanuel Goldenberg   Michael Landon
15. Eugene Orowitz   Danny Kaye

—— SHOW BIZ: TELEVISION ——

A series of quizzes about Jews in entertainment begins with a TV test.

1. Television's biggest deal maker is Jewish. He's _____.
2. And "Arthur Fonzarelli" is Jewish. He's _____.
3. "Mike Stivic" was Jewish too. Who's he?
4. Who was the star of "Your Show of Shows"?
5. And who starred in "You'll Never Get Rich"?
6. "Lou Grant" was a character on the "Mary Tyler Moore" show, played by Jewish actor Ed Asner. What was Lou's job title? Where?
7. Herschel Bernardi played a cop on a hit series of the fifties. Name the series and name the cop.
8. Whose theme songs were "Love in Bloom" and Kreutzer's "Étude No. 1"?

29

9. He produced "The Play of the Week" and "Supermarket Sweep," and became host of his own talk show. Initials: D.S. Who?
10. What non-Jewish columnist-turned-emcee, a Sunday-night fixture on TV, married an Israeli woman?

—— SHOW BIZ: ON STAGE ——

Next, Jews in the theater, from heavy drama to musical comedy to Yiddish plays.

1. The fellow who wrote tunes for Nathan Detroit was Jewish. Who?
2. And the guy who composed for Henry Higgins was Jewish too. Who?
3. Who, in the world of the stage, was known as "Rose Murphisky"?
4. Arthur Miller, the Jewish playwright, won a Pulitzer prize for *Death of a Salesman*. The main character, nearly everyone knows: Willy Loman. But what was Willy's wife's name?
5. Dore Schary's stage story of Franklin D. Roosevelt's triumph over infantile paralysis was titled *Sunrise at Campobello*. What does Schary have FDR doing in the final scene?

6. What river was immortalized in song by the Jewish show team of Oscar Hammerstein and Jerome Kern? In what show?

7. Hammerstein had another Jewish partner for *Oklahoma!* Who?

8. A pair of Jewish writers collaborated on plays titled *Dinner at Eight* and *Stage Door*. Name them.

9. Her acting school became known world-wide: S.A.

10. My name is Lillian. I wrote such plays as *The Children's Hour, The Little Foxes,* and *Toys in the Attic.* Who am I?

11. Name the 1963 play that attacked Pope Pius XII for not making a public condemnation of the Nazis.

12. Probably the most famous Yiddish play is *The Dybbuk,* an early-twentieth-century story of possession, much performed both in the original and in translation. Its author was born Solomon (or Shloyme) Rappoport, but he took a pseudonym. Which was . . . ?

13. *The Dybbuk* is
    A. based on a Jewish legend from medieval Eastern Europe.
    B. based on a Jewish legend from ancient Semitic peoples.
    C. based on a non-Jewish legend from the Orient.
    D. purely the invention of the play's author.

14. Irving Berlin wrote a World War II musical that earned $15 million for army relief. Its name?

15. *Awake and Sing* is the Clifford Odets play about a Jewish family in _____.

16. Who wrote *The Man Who Came to Dinner?*

17. Raised Catholic, she was nonetheless said to have been the daughter of a Jewish prostitute. They called her "divine." She was one of the great names in theater: _____.

18. Elie Wiesel wrote a play about Jews in the Soviet Union. Its title: _____, or *The Madness of God.* Fill in the blank.

19. Who was the Jewish composer of *The Threepenny Opera,* and what was its most famous song?

20. What do these folks have in common: Paul Muni, Molly Picon, Herschel Bernardi, Menasha Skulnik, Edward G. Robinson, and Gertrude Berg.

Here are the names of some plays by the Jewish comedy machine Neil Simon . . . minus a lot of letters. Fill in the titles.

21. T _ _ _   O _ _ _   C _ _ _ _ _ _ _
22. B _ _ _ _ _ _ _ _ _ _ _   I _   T _ _ _   P _ _ _ _
23. C _ _ _ _   B _ _ _ _   Y _ _ _ _   H _ _ _ _
24. P _ _ _ _ _ _   S _ _ _ _ _
25. P _ _ _ _ _ _ _ _ _ _ _   O _   S _ _ _ _ _ _ _
    A _ _ _ _ _ _ _

Answers

1. Frank Loesser (*Guys and Dolls*). 2. Alan Jay Lerner (*My Fair Lady*). 3. That's how Abie Levy introduced his girl friend, Rose Murphy, to his folks in *Abie's Irish Rose*. (They intermarried and lived happily ever after.) 4. Linda. 5. Standing up to nominate Al Smith for Democratic presidential candidate. 6. The Mississippi ("Ol' Man River"), in *Show Boat*. 7. Richard Rodgers. 8. George S. Kaufman and Edna Ferber. 9. Stella Adler. 10. Lillian Hellman. 11. *The Deputy* (by the non-Jewish German playwright Rolf Hochhuth). 12. S. Anski. 13. A. based on a Jewish legend from medieval Eastern Europe. 14. *This Is the Army.* 15. The Bronx. 16. Moss Hart. 17. Sarah Bernhardt. 18. *Zalman.* 19. Kurt Weill, "Mack the Knife." 20. All began in the Yiddish theater. 21. *The Odd Couple.* 22. *Barefoot in the Park.* 23. *Come Blow Your Horn.* 24. *Plaza Suite.* 25. *Prisoner of Second Avenue.*

—— A FIDDLER SAMPLER ——

Fiddler on the Roof deserves its own chapter. Right? Of course right!

1. *Fiddler* was, of course, derived from stories by —————.
2. In what peasant town does the action take place?
3. According to the lyrics of the opening chorus number, "Tradition," at what age do the boys start Hebrew school?
4. What would Tevya do all day long if he were a rich man?
5. And he'd build a house with a roof made of what?
6. In the song "Sabbath Prayer," what two women of the Bible are mentioned?
   A. Ruth and Naomi   C. Ruth and Rebecca
   B. Ruth and Esther   D. Eve and Sarah
7. The girls sing to the matchmaker, describing the men they seek. Naturally, each party to a match has a different idea of what constitutes the perfect fix-up. According to the song, what should the matchmaker find for Poppa? For Momma? And for the girls?
8. Name Lazar Wolf's first wife.
9. Tzeitel's true love is the show nebbech, Motel. What's his last name?
10. This Motel—what does he do for a living? (He isn't the rabbi's son.)
11. What's the name of Hodel's fellow—the young man who's sent to Siberia for political rambunctiousness?
12. Complete: "Why must I travel to a distant land . . ."
13. What's the first response Golde gets to her question "Do you love me?"
14. Which of these has had the starring role in *Fiddler*, on stage or screen?
    A. Topol   C. Herschel Bernardi
    B. Zero Mostel   D. Paul Lipson
               E. Harry Goz

15. When the original Broadway production of *Fiddler* closed, it had beaten out *Life With Father* and *Tobacco Road* for the long-run crown. How many performances had the show tallied?

   A. 1,001   C. 3,242
   B. 2,282   D. 4,995
            E. 18,020

Answers

1. Sholem Aleichem. 2. Anatevka. 3. At three. 4. He'd biddy-biddy-bum. 5. Tin. 6. B. Ruth and Esther. 7. For Poppa: a scholar; for Momma: a man rich as a king; for the girls: a fellow who's handsome as anything. 8. Frumme Sarah. 9. Kamzoil. 10. No—he's a tailor. 11. Perchik. 12. ". . . far from the home I love." 13. "Do I *what?*" 14. All of them. 15. C. 3,242.

—— SHOW BIZ: MOVIES ——

Now twenty-five questions about Jews on and behind the silver screen:

1. What French-Jewish actress won an Academy Award for *Room at the Top* in 1959?
2. Who sang "Lydia the Tattooed Lady" in a 1930s movie? (Bonus: Name the film.)
3. A Jewish actor/comedian played a Danish writer in a children's favorite movie. Who played whom?
4. In the pioneer days of Hollywood, which of these giant companies were run by Jews?
   A. Universal   C. MGM
   B. Paramount   D. Warner Brothers
            E. Loew Theaters
5. Who was Sam Goldfish?

6. Ragtime composer Scott Joplin owes thanks for much of his revival to a young Jewish composer who won an Oscar for turning Joplin material into a movie score. Who's that?

Complete these distinctive names of Jewish film pioneers:

7. Louis B. _____
8. David O. _____
9. Harry, Albert, and Jack _____
10. It was a Jewish movie man—Otto Preminger—who shocked the nation by leaving a certain six-letter word in the film *The Moon Is Blue*. What word?
11. What actor changed his name from Bernard Schwartz and went on to appear in many motion pictures, one notable example being *Some Like it Hot?*
12. French film about an impostor of the cloth: *The Mad Adventures of . . .*
13. What contemporary Jewish actor played a character named Duddy Kravitz and then grew a beard and tackled the shark in *Jaws?*
14. What stentorian-voiced actress, original name Shirley Schrift, won the Oscar for Best Supporting Actress in *The Diary of Anne Frank?*
15. Who, in a popular 1960s movie, was told that the secret of success is "plastics"?

Match the actor to the Jewish music man he portrayed in films:

16. Jerome Kern	Steve Allen
17. George Gershwin	Mickey Rooney
18. Benny Goodman	Robert Walker
19. Eddie Cantor	Larry Parks
20. Al Jolson	Robert Alda
21. Lorenz Hart	Keefe Brasselle

22. Paulette Goddard, herself Jewish, played a Jewish role in a Charlie Chaplin film. Which one?
23. Every serious film fanatic knows *Citizen Kane*. And every serious film fanatic knows its Jewish writer. Do you?

24. That man's brother was also in the movie business. He's best known for directing a 1963 epic starring Elizabeth Taylor and Richard Burton. His name and the film's, please?
25. Two Jewish actors were involved in this history-making episode: After A starred as the cantor's son in the stage version of this show, he was offered the role in a film version, destined to go down in history as the "first talkie." But A demanded too much money, so B got the role and the spot in history. Who were A and B? And the show?

Answers

1. Simone Signoret. 2. Groucho Marx. (Bonus: *At the Circus.*) 3. Danny Kaye played Hans Christian Andersen in the movie named for the fairy-tale great. 4. All of them. 5. Sam Goldwyn (who changed his name and became a co-founder of MGM). 6. Marvin Hamlisch (*The Sting*). 7. Mayer. 8. Selznick. 9. Warner. 10. "Virgin." 11. Tony Curtis. 12. . . . "*Rabbi" Jacob.* 13. Richard Dreyfuss. 14. Shelley Winters. 15. Dustin Hoffman, in *The Graduate.* 16. Kern—Robert Walker. 17. Gershwin—Robert Alda. 18. Goodman—Steve Allen. 19. Cantor—Keefe Brasselle. 20. Jolson—Larry Parks. 21. Hart—Mickey Rooney. 22. *The Great Dictator.* 23. Herman Mankiewicz. 24. Joseph Mankiewicz, *Cleopatra.* 25. A was Georgie Jessel, B was Al Jolson, and the show, of course, was *The Jazz Singer.*

A VERY FUNNY
—— WORD-FIND PUZZLE ——

You'll find the names of twenty Jewish funny men and women in this grid. Their names are left to right (like English), right to left (like Hebrew), top to bottom (like Chinese), bottom to top (like Chinese backwards), and even diagonal (like shikker). Use a pencil to circle them.

```
P  R  D  E  B  R  O  S  I  D  C  A  E  S  A  R
F  R  J  E  T  L  S  A  G  A  I  R  N  H  Z  E
U  M  A  J  S  M  L  M  E  V  N  E  S  E  Y  D
R  M  A  A  C  A  L  L  O  I  I  T  K  L  O  B
I  Y  B  C  N  R  Y  E  R  D  A  R  R  L  E  U
T  R  S  K  R  T  B  V  G  S  M  A  I  Y  D  T
W  O  I  I  E  Y  T  E  E  T  R  C  A  B  R  T
E  N  B  E  N  A  S  N  B  E  A  K  S  E  A  O
G  C  U  M  I  L  E  S  U  I  Y  C  P  R  N  N
R  O  D  A  R  L  N  O  R  N  H  A  O  M  O  S
P  H  D  S  B  E  I  N  N  B  I  J  O  A  E  O
I  E  Y  O  E  N  B  A  S  E  Y  A  C  N  L  C
N  N  H  N  S  U  D  O  N  R  I  C  K  L  E  S
A  M  A  I  H  O  B  J  O  G  I  D  E  F  K  Y
N  U  C  Y  S  R  E  V  I  R  N  A  O  J  C  K
O  M  K  N  I  E  L  K  T  R  E  B  O  R  A  O
C  O  E  P  H  I  L  S  I  L  V  E  R  S  J  R
F  L  T  H  E  N  N  Y  Y  O  U  N  G  M  A  N
H  A  T  P  A  M  P  O  H  S  I  B  Y  E  O  J
```

37

```
P R D E B R O S I D C A E S A R
F R J E T L S A G A I R N H Z E
U M A J S M L M E V N E S E Y D
R M A A C A L L O I I T K L O B
I Y B C N R Y E R D A R R L E U
T R S K R T B V G S M A I Y D T
W O I I E Y T E E T R C A B R T
E N B E N A S N B E A K S E A O
G C U M I L E S U I Y C P R N N
R O D A R L N O R N H A O M O S
P H D S B E I N N B I J O A E O
I E Y O E N B A S E Y A C N L C
N N H N S U D O N R I C K L E S
A M A I H O B J O G I D E F K Y
N U C Y S R E V I R N A O J C K
O M K N I E L K T R E B O R A O
C O E P H I L S I L V E R S J R
F L T H E N N Y Y O U N G M A N
H A T P A M P O H S I B Y E O J
```

Horizontal: SID CAESAR, DON RICKLES, JOAN RIVERS, ROBERT KLEIN, PHIL SILVERS, HENNY YOUNGMAN, JOEY BISHOP *Vertical:* MYRON COHEN, BUDDY HACKETT, JACKIE MASON, MARTY ALLEN, SAM LEVENSON, GEORGE BURNS, DAVID STEINBERG, JACK CARTER, SHELLY BERMAN, JACK E. LEONARD, RED BUTTONS *Diagonal:* ALAN KING, DANNY KAYE

Answers

―― ALL BUT TWO ――

On this list, everyone's in show business. Everyone's Jewish, too
. . . except two. Can you pick out the two?

1.	Carl Reiner	7.	Allen Funt
2.	Leonard Nimoy	8.	Valerie Harper
3.	Steve Allen	9.	Lorne Greene
4.	Bill Macy	10.	Beatrice Arthur
5.	Bob Dylan	11.	George Segal
6.	Susan Strasberg	12.	Barry Manilow

Answers

3. and 8., Steve Allen and Valerie Harper, aren't Jewish.

―― MORE JEWISH COMEDIANS ――

This puzzle has clues, each of which describes a Jewish comic.
When you have the names, transfer the numbered letters to the
right boxes and you'll spell a mystery phrase.

1. Wrote *What's New, Pussycat?* __ __ __ __
                    3 8 8 11

__ __ __ __ __
13   2 14

2. Wrote *The Producers.* __ __ __ __ __ __ __ __ __
                    9 10   8 8   5

3. Often dressed in drag. __ __ __ __ __ __ __ __ __ __ __
                   9 4   8 14   2   10

4. Dino's one-time partner. __ __ __ __ __ __ __ __ __
                    1 2   10 3 12 15

5. The one, the only. ___ ___ ___ ___ ___ ___ ___ ___ ___
        8   7 6 8   9 13

1	2	3	4	5	6		7	8	9	10	11	12	13	14	15

Answers

—— SHOW BIZ: POTPOURRI ——

A short hodgepodge of questions about Jews in the world of entertainment.

1. What funny Jewish lady calls her hubby "Fang"?
2. What hip-Jewish-intellectual comic became a latter-day Will Rogers, carrying a rolled-up newspaper on stage for his monologue about current events?
3. Very fat, Jewish, initials T.F. Who was that?
4. Jack Benny once said, "One of the nicest eulogies I ever heard him deliver was about one of James Mason's cats. I *never knew* that cat had done *so much* for Israel." He could have said it about only one man. Who?
5. Speaking of Jack: Who, on his radio show, used to say, "Vell, hallo, Mr. Benny!" with a heavy Yiddish accent?
6. The Jew widely considered the finest mime of our time has the same initials as a famous cartoon rodent. Name the mime.

7. She was a vaudeville sensation. Her trademarks were a fan and a lace handkerchief. She was born Leonora Goldberg. She was known as _____.
8. One of the most successful talent managers in the history of show business: Brian Epstein. Whom did he bring to fame?
9. The name of Orson Welles is of course associated with the famous "Mercury Theater" radio production of *The War of the Worlds*—the 1939 Halloween broadcast that panicked many listeners. Welles ran the show, but a Jewish writer did the script. Do you know him?
10. Walter Matthau played the slob sportswriter in *The Odd Couple* on stage and screen. What's the character's name?

Answers

1. Phyllis Diller. 2. Mort Sahl. 3. Totie Fields. 4. George Jessel. 5. Mr. Kitzel (Artie Auerbach). 6. Marcel Marceau. 7. Nora Bayes. 8. The Beatles. 9. Howard Koch. 10. Oscar Madison.

—— SONGS AND SUCH ——

Some musical miscellany.

1. What Jewish entrepreneur was responsible for the sixties rock showcases Fillmore East and Fillmore West?
2. Name the lively Israeli tune that became a big hit in the U.S.A. in 1950. (Hint: four-word title, all four the same.)
3. George Gershwin wrote a famous jazz concerto for piano. In what key?
4. Which *didn't* George Gershwin compose?
   A. *Billy the Kid*   C. *An American in Paris*
   B. *Of Thee I Sing*   D. *Porgy and Bess*
          E. *Rhapsody in Blue*

5. What Jewish pianist/raconteur was most closely associated with Gershwin?
6. Novelty song title: "Sam, You Made . . ."
7. Another: "Yiddle . . ."
8. "Zum Gali Gali" tells about "hechalutz." What's that?
9. According to Eddie Fisher, what should you do when you're worried and you can't sleep? (And what'll happen?)
10. Which *didn't* Leonard Bernstein compose?

    A. *On the Town*   C. *Three Places in New England*
    B. *West Side Story*   D. *Kaddish*

11. I should say "bella, bella" or "wunderbar" but I'd rather sing it in Yiddish. What shall I sing?
12. According to the song, what happens when the rebbe dances?
13. Would you describe the Rebbe Elimelech as happy or sad?
14. What Jewish pianist formed one of the most important modern jazz quartets?
15. With which festival do you associate the song "Addir Hu"?
16. What musician first played in a Chicago synagogue and is now the jazzman most closely identified with Carnegie Hall?
17. What's the usual translation of the song title "Maoz Tzur"?
18. Although later converted to Catholicism, this young singer was born of a Jewish mother and a very famous folk-singing father. (He had what he calls "the world's first hootenanny bar mitzvah.") He wrote a smash song about his arrest for littering and his subsequent run-in with the draft office. The song became a movie, in which he played himself. Name the big song and the big singer.
19. Who told about a summer at Camp Granada in a letter-song to his parents?
20. What favorite song of the Yiddish theater tells of a calf being brought to market, a bird flying overhead, and the winds laughing?
21. What patriotic Jewish-American wrote the flag-waving World War II song, "God Bless America"?

Match the Jewish composer to the song:

22. Irving Berlin   "Over the Rainbow"
23. Gus Kahn   "God Bless America"
24. Harold Arlen   "Raindrops Keep Falling on My Head"
25. Burt Bacharach   "Carolina in the Morning"

Answers

1. Bill Graham. 2. "Tzena, Tzena, Tzena." 3. F. 4. A. 5. Billy the Kid (by another Jewish composer, Aaron Copland). 6. ". . . the Pants Too Long." 7. ". . . on Your Fiddle." 8. The pioneer. 9. You should count your blessings instead of sheep—and you'll have a very good night's sleep, take my word for it. 10. C. Three Places in New England (by Charles Ives). 11. "Bei Mir Bist Du Shayn." 12. All the Chasidim dance too. ("Az der rebbe tanzt, tanzt men alle Chasidim.") 13. Freylach-happy. 14. Dave Brubeck. 15. Passover. 16. Benny Goodman. 17. "Rock of Ages." 18. "Alice's Restaurant"; Arlo Guthrie. 19. Allan Sherman. 20. "Dana, Dana, Dana." 21. Irving Berlin. 22. Berlin—"God Bless America." 23. Kahn—"Carolina in the Morning." 24. Arlen—"Over the Rainbow." 25. Bacharach—"Raindrops Keep Falling on My Head."

—— MUSIC: ON THE HEAVY SIDE ——

Take five questions on more serious music.

1. The can-can man was Jewish. Who was he?
2. He wrote symphonies titled *Israel* and *America*, a cello piece called *Shelomoh,* and a Sabbath composition, *Avodat ha-Kodesh.* He was a Swiss-American Jew who died in 1959. Who was he?
3. Born Jacob Liebmann Beer, he was a piano prodigy and developed into an important composer of operas: G.M.
4. The most jazz-influenced member of the composers' group Les Six was a Jew who wrote several Jewish-oriented works, including *Chants populaires hébraïques, Hymne de Sion, Poèmes juifs,* and others. Name him.
5. Modest Moussorgsky, though not Jewish, wrote a suite with a movement portraying two Jews in a small Polish town. First, name the piece; second, for a bonus point, give the title of the movement and you'll name the two Jews.

Answers

1. Jacques Offenbach, composer of *The Tales of Hoffmann* and other pieces. 2. Ernest Bloch. 3. Giacomo Meyerbeer. 4. Darius Milhaud. 5. *Pictures at an Exhibition;* Samuel Goldenburg and Schmuyle. (Samuel, the rich Jew, is represented by lower strings; Schmuyle, the poor Jew, by a muted trumpet.)

44

HAVE YOU HEARD
THIS ONE?

It's the High Holy Days, and the synagogue, naturally, is packed like a jar of herring. Up rushes a man, who is stopped at the door by the shammes demanding, "Ticket, please."

"What ticket?" asks the man. "I have no ticket. I'm just looking for my brother, Abe."

"Sorry," he is told. "On Rosh Hashonah you have to have a ticket."

"Please!" the man begs. "It's an important matter. I've *got* to see my brother! I'll only be a minute."

"Are you sure it's important?" asks the shammes.

"Absolutely!" answers the man. "Very important, I swear!"

"Well, okay," says the shammes sternly, "for just a minute. But _____
_____!"

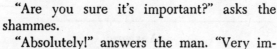 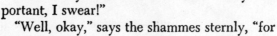 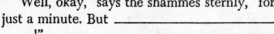

"... don't let me catch you praying!"

45

——— MUSIC MAKERS ———

Jewish music men and women all. Identify and match.

1.	Shlomo Carlebach	jazz trumpeter
2.	Larry Adler	cellist
3.	Shorty Rogers	harpsichordist
4.	King David	opera tenor
5.	Jan Peerce	harmonica player
6.	Roberta Peters	cantor
7.	Wanda Landowska	harp player
8.	Jascha Heifetz	folk singer
9.	Theodore Bikel	violinist
10.	Gregor Piatigorsky	opera soprano

Answers

1. Carlebach—cantor 2. Adler—harmonica player 3. Rogers—jazz trumpeter 4. David—harp player 5. Peerce—opera tenor 6. Peters—opera soprano 7. Landowska—harpsichordist 8. Heifetz—violinist 9. Bikel—folk singer 10. Piatigorsky—cellist

---

——— MORE MUSIC MAKERS... ———

Who doesn't belong on this list of Jewish musicians, and why?

A. Vladimir Horowitz   D. Arthur Rubinstein
B. Rudolf Serkin   E. Erich Leinsdorf
C. Peter Serkin   F. Dame Myra Hess
     G. Artur Schnabel

—— . . .AND MORE ——

Who doesn't belong here?

A. Morton Gould

B. Meyer Davis

C. Daniel Barenboim

D. Eugene Ormandy

E. Arthur Fiedler

F. André Kostelanetz

G. Bruno Walter

Answer

C. Daniel Barenboim is a pianist; the others are—or were—conductors.

—— THE ART WORLD ——

How much do you know about art and artists? This artful quiz deals with painters, sculptors, cartoonists, patrons, and even subjects. Try it.

1. Where is there *not* an example of Chagall stained glass?
   A. Hadassah Medical Center, Jerusalem
   B. Westminster Abbey
   C. The United Nations
   D. The Vatican
   E. The Paris Opera House

2. What Russian-American Jewish artist is known for his illustration of the Passover Haggadah?
3. Who's this great painter? Early 1900s . . . instantly recognizable style . . . favored nudes and portraits, particularly of long-necked, almond-eyed women . . . a Jew born in Italy.
4. One of the founders of Impressionism was a Sephardic Jew born in the West Indies. In Paris and London he painted landscapes and scenes of street life. Who?
5. In what city can you find Michelangelo's statue of the young Jewish hero David?
6. Who was the Jewish cartoonist whose name made it into the dictionary, defining a wacky, complicated invention or contraption?
7. Another Jewish cartoonist is known for embedding his daughter's name in his drawings, driving his fans meshuggeh, making them squint until they find the hidden names. Name father and daughter both.
8. This major painter wasn't Jewish, but he lived in his city's Jewish quarter and did numerous portraits of Jews. "The Jewish Bride" was one of his last great works. "Woman Cutting Her Nails," showing a woman preparing for the mikveh, is another of his. Who was he?
9. One of New York's most distinctive museums is as famous for its own spiraling architecture as for its art collection. Name the Jewish industrialist and patron of the arts whose name it carries.
10. And who's the Jewish art collector whose name graces a circular, windowless museum in Washington, D.C., with a dazzling collection inside?

Match the first names to last and come up with five Jewish artists of this century.

11. George	Epstein
12. Jacques	Soyer
13. Raphael	Segal
14. Jacob	Lipchitz
15. Chaim	Gross

—— FROM THE BOOKSHELF ——

Questions about Jewish authors and books of all sorts.

1. What Jewish-American author wrote popular historical novels based on the lives of Vincent Van Gogh and Michelangelo? And name the two books.
2. He wrote the first big World War II novel, which included the characters of two Jewish soldiers. He's Jewish himself. He's tough and very famous. The book's title looks like this: *The _____ and the _____.* Got it?
3. Who, in the world of literature, was Solomon Rabinovitz?
4. Nelson Algren wrote a novel that became a fifties movie with a popular jazz score. The story was one of drugs and degeneracy. Name it.
5. Give the title and the non-Jewish French author of the celebrated open letter to the President of France about the Dreyfus affair.
6. What was the subject of *Gentleman's Agreement?*
7. This Jewish journalist is best known for his series of books chronicling presidential election campaigns, beginning with 1960. Name him.
8. Name the first Hebrew writer to win a Nobel Prize in Literature, in 1966.
9. The Hebrew laureate shared the big prize that year with another Jewish writer—a German-born poet living in Sweden, initials N.S. Can you name her?

10. A bit of cake and a cup of tea led to a multivolume work of some one and a half million words. The author was a European Jew. Who? (And what kind of cake did he dunk?)
11. In *What Makes Sammy Run?* by Budd Schulberg, what's Sammy's last name? (It starts with G.)
12. Stephen Birmingham (not Jewish) wrote a best-selling account of "the great Jewish families of New York"—people with such names as Schiff and Kahn and Lehman and Lewisohn and Loeb and Warburg and Guggenheim and Straus. Name the book.
13. This writer had a No. 1 best seller. Then he followed with *For 2¢ Plain, Enjoy, Enjoy*, and others. Name the writer and his first hit.
14. Can you describe K'tonton, the hero of a well-known Jewish children's tale?
15. If someone spoke cryptically about Bennett C., Alfred K., and Max S., would you know that you were hearing about Jewish publishers? Would you know the names of the three firms they founded?

The Jewish Initials Game (Books Division):

16. Author of *How to Be a Jewish Mother*: D.G.
17. Author of *The Adventures of Augie March*: S.B.
18. Author of *The World of Our Fathers*: I.H.
19. Author of *Lummox, Back Street*, and *Great Laughter*: F.H.
20. Author of *The Caine Mutiny*: H.W.

Hurst. 20. Herman Wouk.
Greenburg. 17. Saul Bellow. 18. Irving Howe. 19. Fannie
A. Knopf, Inc.; Max Lincoln Schuster, of Simon & Schuster. 16. Dan
brew.) 15. Bennett Cerf, of Random House; Alfred Knopf, of Alfred
he's the Jewish Tom Thumb. (In fact, the name means tiny in He-
13. Harry Golden, *Only in America*. 14. Small, very small—
Past). (He ate *petites madeleines*.) 11. Click. 12. *Our Crowd*.
Proust (*À la recherche du temps perdu—Remembrance of Things
quadrennial sequels). 8. S. Y. Agnon. 9. Nelly Sachs. 10. Marcel
Theodore H. White (*The Making of the President* 1960 and its
J'accuse by Emile Zola. 6. Anti-Jewish sentiment in the U.S.A. 7.
Twain," Sholem Aleichem. 4. *The Man With the Golden Arm*. 5.
Norman Mailer (*The Naked and the Dead*). 3. "The Jewish Mark
2. Irving Stone; *Lust for Life* and *The Agony and the Ecstasy*.

JEWISH CHARACTERS OF FICTION

Shakespeare's Shylock wasn't the only Jewish character created by a non-Jewish author. Here are questions about just five more.

1. Who created the character of Fagin, a cunning Jew who lived off the money stolen by children under his tutelage?
2. And what American author of the twenties wrote about a German-Jewish medical researcher, Dr. Max Gottlieb?
3. Ernest Hemingway wrote about a Jewish chap named Robert Cohn in a novel that takes its title from Ecclesiastes. Name the Hemingway title.
4. His name was Bloom and he lived in Dublin. What was the book? (Bonus: What was Bloom's first name?)
5. What classic English novel includes a Jewish moneylender called Isaac of York and his daughter Rebecca, who is accused of being a witch and rescued by the hero?

51

Answers

1. Charles Dickens, in *Oliver Twist*. 2. Sinclair Lewis, in *Arrow-smith*. 3. *The Sun Also Rises*. 4. James Joyce's *Ulysses*. (Bonus: Leopold.) 5. *Ivanhoe*, by Sir Walter Scott.

—— WHAT DID THE RABBI ——
DO TODAY?

If you read modern fiction, you've probably gone through at least a couple of Harry Kemelman's "rabbi" series: *Friday the Rabbi Slept Late*, etc. So can you put together these five titles?

1. *Saturday the Rabbi . . .*   *. . . Took Off*
2. *Sunday the Rabbi . . .*   *. . . Got Wet*
3. *Monday the Rabbi . . .*   *. . . Went Hungry*
4. *Tuesday the Rabbi . . .*   *. . . Stayed Home*
5. *Wednesday the Rabbi . . .*   *. . . Saw Red*

Answers

1. *Saturday the Rabbi Went Hungry* 2. *Sunday the Rabbi Stayed Home* 3. *Monday the Rabbi Took Off* 4. *Tuesday the Rabbi Saw Red* 5. *Wednesday the Rabbi Got Wet*

—— TEN OPENING LINES... ——

All these sentences begin famous books by Jewish authors.

1. Sunday, 14 June, 1942. On Friday, June 12th, I woke up at six o'clock and no wonder; it was my birthday.
2. Someone must have traduced Joseph K., for without having done anything wrong he was arrested one fine morning.
3. The first time I saw Brenda, she asked me to hold her glasses.
4. It was love at first sight. The first time Yossarian saw the chaplain he fell madly in love with him.
5. Mr. Donnelly, the track coach, ended the day's practice early because Henry Fuller's father came down to the high-school field to tell Henry that they had just got a telegram from Washington announcing that Henry's brother had been killed in action in Germany.
6. Customs of courtship vary greatly in different times and places, but the way the thing happens to be done here and now always seems the only natural way to do it.

   Marjorie's mother looked in on her sleeping daughter at half past ten of a Sunday morning with feelings of puzzlement and dread.
7. *November 1946*
   ### WELCOME TO CYPRUS
   WILLIAM SHAKESPEARE

   The airplane plip-plopped down the runway to a halt before the big sign: WELCOME TO CYPRUS. Mark Parker looked out of the window and in the distance he could see . . .
8. From the small crossed window of his room above the stable in the brickyard, Yakov Bok saw people in their long overcoats running somewhere early that morning, everybody in the same direction. Vey iz mir, he thought uneasily, something bad has happened.

53

9. September, 1945. The temperature hit ninety degrees the day she arrived. New York was steaming—an angry concrete animal caught unawares in an unseasonable hot spell. But she didn't mind the heat or the littered midway called Times Square. She thought New York was the most exciting city in the world.

10. There were 117 psychoanalysts on the Pan Am flight to Vienna and I'd been treated by at least six of them. And married to a seventh.

Now, if you've had trouble, you'll find the answers in this list:

Valley of the Dolls, by Jacqueline Susann
The Trial, by Franz Kafka
Rich Man, Poor Man, by Irwin Shaw
Marjorie Morningstar, by Herman Wouk
Goodbye, Columbus, by Philip Roth
The Fixer, by Bernard Malamud
Fear of Flying, by Erica Jong
Exodus, by Leon Uris
Catch-22, by Joseph Heller
Anne Frank: The Diary of a Young Girl

Answers

1. *Anne Frank: The Diary of a Young Girl.* 2. *The Trial.* 3. *Goodbye, Columbus.* 4. *Catch-22.* 5. *Rich Man, Poor Man.* 6. *Marjorie Morningstar.* 7. *Exodus.* 8. *The Fixer.* 9. *Valley of the Dolls.* 10. *Fear of Flying.*

HAVE YOU HEARD
THIS ONE?

A Martian spaceship lands on the Lower East Side, right in the street. Two little green men emerge, each with three eyes and a tail. They march into a bakery.

"What are those little wheels in the window?" asks one Martian of Ostrovsky the baker.

"Wheels?" laughs Ostrovsky. "Those ain't wheels—they're bagels, to eat. I guess where you come from, you don't know from bagels. Here—try an onion bagel."

The first Martian sinks his teeth in and smacks his lips. The second Martian does the same.

"Hey, delicious!" says the first Martian to his pal. "I'll say!" agrees the second. "_____
_____?"

"And wouldn't this go great with cream cheese and lox?"

Which you certainly should know.

"So [*said the doctor*]. Now vee may perhaps to begin. Yes?"

Answer

Portnoy's Complaint, by Philip Roth.

—— **QUESTIONS POETIC** ——

Do you think that you know poems best?
Well, then, this is just your kind of test.

1. Here are some lines from a famous sonnet of the nineteenth century:

    "Keep, ancient lands, your storied pomp!" cries she
    With silent lips. "Give me your tired, your poor,
    Your huddled masses yearning to breathe free,
    The wretched refuse of your teeming shore. . . .

    A. Complete the sonnet.
    B. Name the Jewish poet who wrote it.
    C. Tell where the poem is inscribed.
2. Who wrote poems called *Howl* and *Kaddish for Naomi Ginsberg (1894–1956)*?
3. Who was the great German poet often set to music, by such as Schubert, Schumann, and Mendelssohn, Jewish born but converted?

4. An early American poet, not Jewish, wrote "The Jewish Cemetery at Newport." Who was it?
5. Robert Browning wrote a poem about a Spanish rabbi. The title is one of these:

   A. *Rabbi Mordecai*   C. *Rabbi Ben Segovia*
   B. *Rabbi Ben Ezra*   D. *The Rabbi of Toledo*
           E. *Reb Oded*

Answers

1. A. Send these, the homeless, tempest-tost, to me: I lift my lamp beside the golden door!" B. Emma Lazarus. C. In the base of the Statue of Liberty. 2. Her son, Allen Ginsberg. 3. Heinrich Heine. 4. Henry Wadsworth Longfellow. 5. B. *Rabbi Ben Ezra.*

—— SCIENCE AND MEDICINE ——

Here are questions about a bunch of little Jewish boys who grew up to be "my son the doctor" or "my son the research biochemist." Their mothers knew all about their work. Do you?

1. How old was Albert Einstein when he developed the theory of relativity?

   A. 16   C. 50
   B. 26   D. 81

2. In 1939, Einstein wrote a letter to Franklin D. Roosevelt that persuaded the President to take an action that changed world history. What did Einstein propose?
3. I developed a vaccine for a paralytic disease that once produced widespread fear and pain. Now, thanks to shots of the fluid commonly called by my name, the fear and pain are under control. Who am I?
4. I also came up with a vaccine—for the very same dread disease. But my vaccine is taken orally. Who am I?

57

5. Edison invented a cylinder talking machine, called the pho-
nograph. A Jew named Emile Berliner invented a disk talking machine, called . . . ?
6. With what contraption do you connect Edward Teller?
7. I wrote a book called *The Interpretation of Dreams*. That's
not all I did, but if I tell you much more I'll be handing you
the answer on a silver platter. Who am I?
8. I lived in the twelfth century. I am best remembered for my
studies and writings on Jewish law and thought, but I was a
physician in Cairo. I have been called "the Jewish Aristotle."
Who am I?
9. William Herschel was an eighteenth-century Jewish astron-
omer who discovered the first planet found in modern times.
Name the planet.
10. Before he became a noted Zionist leader, Chaim Weizmann
was a scientist. In what field?
11. A sixteenth-century Frenchman of Jewish descent, I was ap-
pointed physician to King Charles IX, who was impressed
with my record of forecasting future events. People still read
my predictions today. Who am I?
12. Radio stations often announce their frequencies with a term
named for the physicist of Jewish descent who first discovered radio waves. What's the term? And who was he?
13. I was a German-Jewish bacteriologist and medical man.
Three quarters of a century ago, I created a test still used
today to detect syphilis. The test bears my name. Who am I?
14. I also developed a test now named for me—this one to identify diphtheria. Who am I?
15. I was a German-Jewish scientist—a biochemist. My big dis-
covery was a cure for syphilis, which won me a Nobel prize.
A Jewish actor—Edward G. Robinson—played me in a
movie of my successful search for the cure. Who am I?
16. With what southwestern city do you identify J. Robert Op-
penheimer?
17. I broke away from my Jewish mentor (he overdid the sex
bit, I thought) and pushed my own theory of individual psy-
chology. Who am I?
18. Casimir Funk was a Polish-Jewish biochemist who discov-

ered things everyone has and knows about. We call them by
letters and numbers. What?

19. Tay-Sachs disease is a fatal disorder of the central nervous
system that occurs chiefly among
    A. persons of Mediterranean ancestry
    B. Jews of Eastern European extraction
    C. Sephardic Jews
    D. Jews and blacks
    E. American Jews
20. What's "Jewish penicillin"?

Answers

1. *B.* 26. 2. That the United States undertake a crash program to construct an atomic bomb before the enemy built one. 3. Jonas Salk (polio vaccine). 4. Albert Sabin. 5. The Gramophone. 6. The hydrogen bomb. 7. Sigmund Freud. 8. Moses Maimonides. 9. The seventh: Uranus. 10. Chemistry. 11. Nostradamus. 12. The term is hertz (or kilohertz), and the scientist was Heinrich Rudolf Hertz. 13. August von Wassermann. 14. Béla Schick. 15. Paul Ehrlich. (The movie: *Dr. Ehrlich's Magic Bullet.*) 16. Los Alamos, New Mexico, site of the Los Alamos Project, the effort that produced the first atomic bomb. 17. Alfred Adler. 18. Vitamins. 19. *B.* Jews of Eastern European extraction. 20. Sure, it's that old cure-all: chicken soup.

—— HIGH SCHOLARSHIP ——

Some questions for the intellectual set. If you can't answer them,
don't feel bad. Could Einstein make a kugel? Could he spin a
dreydl, even? No one can be good at everything.

1. What famous Dutch-Jewish philosopher was excommunicated for heresy? (The act was voided centuries later.)

59

2. This German's parents were Jewish (both his grandfathers were rabbis, in fact), but he was baptized as a child and was less than fond of Jews. He grew up to become one of the most influential men of the nineteenth century, and his force is felt even today. His main writing is a three-volume economic critique that is among the world's most widely translated works. Got it yet?

3. The word "phenomenology," if you know it well, should bring to mind another German philosopher, Jewish by birth but not by upbringing, initials E.H. Who?

4. It took this man awhile, but he turned the world of linguistics upside down with his book *Syntactic Structures*. Later he became better known as a critic of the War in Vietnam. Who is he?

5. Name the neo-Freudian psychoanalyst who wrote *The Art of Loving*.

6. Who wrote *Guide for the Perplexed?*

7. What critic was known for studies of Matthew Arnold and E. M. Forster and other works titled *The Liberal Imagination, Freud and the Crisis of Our Culture*, and *Beyond Culture?*

8. And who wrote *A Preface to Politics* and *A Preface to Morals?*

9. What twentieth-century Jewish philosopher wrote *I and Thou*, a major work on the dialogue between man and God, a book that has influenced Christian theologians as well as Jews?

10. If you were reading philosophical works that spoke of intellect, intuition, duration, and the *élan vital*, whose writings would you be reading?

11. What was Edward Sapir's field?

12. He was an important German-Jewish thinker of the 1800s. He translated the Bible into German, argued for Jewish freedom, and, for his philosophical writings, became known as "the Jewish Plato." Still, today he's most recognized as the grandfather of a notable composer. Who was he?

13. Two famous Jewish sociologists: Erik _____ and Émile _____.

14. Two famous Jewish anthropologists: _____ Boas and _____ Lévi-Strauss.

15. The best-known Jewish Bible commentator was Shlomo Ben Isaac, better known as _____.

Answers

HAVE YOU HEARD
THIS ONE?

 Mendel the Shnorrer stands with his hand out. Along comes Menahem the Trader and puts a kopeck in it.

"Hey!" shouts Mendel. "You always give me two kopecks. How come only one today?"

"Listen, Mendel," pleads Menahem. "Business is bad. That's all I can afford."

"So," says Mendel irritated, "_____?"

"... because you've got problems, I should suffer?"

— NOBEL PRIZES —

1. Did Albert Einstein win a Nobel prize?
2. What Jewish writer declined the Nobel Literature award in 1958?
3. The 1973 Peace Prize was awarded jointly to an Oriental and an American Jew. Who was the Jew?
4. Selman Abraham Waksman won a Nobel for developing an antibiotic used for TB and other diseases. Was it
    A. penicillin?   C. erythromycin?
    B. streptomycin?   D. neomycin?
                E. kanamycin?
5. Do you think more Jews have won Nobel awards in physics, medicine and physiology, chemistry, peace, literature, or economics?

Match the laureates with their fields:

6. Paul Samuelson (1970)   physics
7. Salvador Luria (1969)   physics
8. Isidor Isaac Rabi (1944)   economics
9. Milton Friedman (1976)   economics
10. Niels Bohr (1922)   medicine and physiology

Answers

1. Yes, in 1921. 2. Boris Pasternak. 3. Henry Kissinger, U. S. Secretary of State. (His co-winner, Le Duc Tho, of North Vietnam, declined the award.) 4. B. Streptomycin. 5. The medicine prizes have it. 6. Economics. 7. Medicine and physiology. 8. Physics. 9. Economics. 10. Physics.

—— IN PUBLIC LIFE ——

A quiz on Jews in governments past and present, here and there.

1. Arthur Goldberg served as U.S. ambassador to the United
   Nations, associate justice of the U. S. Supreme Court, and
   Secretary of Labor. In what order?
2. Robert Briscoe became the darling of American Jews when
   he was elected Lord Mayor of Dublin. How many times did
   he serve in that post?
3. How many times was Herbert Lehman elected governor of
   New York State?
4. Which *hasn't* Jacob Javits been: senator, congressman, attor-
   ney general of New York State, federal judge?
5. Who was the member of an old-line Jewish family in France
   who served briefly as French Premier in 1954–55, negotiat-
   ing an end to the fighting in Indochina?
6. Can you name the Jewish U.S. senator who withdrew in 1861
   and joined Jefferson Davis's Confederate Cabinet, first as At-
   torney General, then as Secretary of War, then as the Confederacy's final Secretary of State?
7. Who was the first Jewish justice on the U. S. Supreme Court?
   Which President chose him?
8. His real name was Lev Davidovich Bronstein, but fellow
   fans of the Russian Revolution knew him by another name.
   So does history. So do you, if you can just think of it. Can
   you?
9. Who was "the Disraeli of South Africa"?
10. U. S. Presidents haven't much time to write their own words,
    so they have others write them. It was Jewish writers who
    came up with the biggest slogans of Presidents FDR and
    LBJ. First, give the slogans. Then (much harder) name the
    writers.
11. What cabinet post did Henry M. Morgenthau, Jr., hold dur-
    ing the New Deal? (Bonus: What non-government job did
    he hold afterward?)

63

12. What two major posts in government did Ernest Gruening hold?
13. Name the Jewish congressman who served a quarter century and chaired the House Foreign Affairs Committee through much of the forties.
14. What bright young Jewish lawyer catapulted to fame as counsel at the televised Army-McCarthy hearings?
15. What Jewish man's signature is on U.S. currency dated 1977?

The Jewish Initials Game (Politics Division):

16. First Jewish head of the Big Apple: A.B.
17. New England senator: A.R.
18. Lady of the hats, in D.C.: B.A.
19. "Whiz kid" in the Carter Cabinet: H.B.
20. Pipe-smoking money watcher: A.B.

Answers

1. Reverse: Secretary of Labor under JFK in 1961–62, on the High Court in 1962–65, at the UN in 1965–66. 2. Twice: 1956–57 and 1961–62. 3. Three. 4. A judge he wasn't. 5. Pierre Mendès-France. 6. Judah P. Benjamin. 7. Louis D. Brandeis; Woodrow Wilson. 8. Leon Trotsky. 9. Saul Solomon, head of the Liberal Party in the Cape Parliament. 10. "New Deal" and "Great Society"; Samuel Rosenman and Richard Goodwin. 11. Secretary of the Treasury. (Bonus: He was general chairman of the UJA and then U.S. chairman of the Israel bond drive.) 12. Governor of and senator from Alaska. 13. Sol Bloom. 14. Roy Cohn. 15. W. Michael Blumenthal, Secretary of the Treasury. 16. Abraham Beame, first Jewish mayor of New York. 17. Abraham Ribicoff, senator from Connecticut. 18. Bella Abzug, ex-congresswoman with hats trademark. 19. Harold Brown, Secretary of Defense. 20. Arthur Burns, former chairman of the Federal Reserve Board.

—— JEWS IN BUSINESS ——

Although Jews in business have historically been of the mom-and-pop variety, some became denizens of the upper strata. Here are fifteen questions about some of them.

1. Millions wear an item named for a nineteenth-century Bavarian Jew who came to America and struck it rich in the clothing industry. Who's that?
2. The five sons of Rothschild set up business in five European cities. Which five?

   A. London   D. Frankfurt
   B. Paris   E. Naples
   C. Vienna   F. Zurich
3. What did Edward and Lincoln Filene do?
4. Benjamin Altman, of department-store success, is noted for having donated

   A. cash to the Guggenheim Museum
   B. art to the Metropolitan Museum
   C. clothing to earthquake victims
   D. $1 million to Planned Parenthood
5. Louis Blaustein formed the American Oil Company, which his son Jacob later controlled. Its better-known trade name?
6. What was the name of the family that took over Macy's department store in 1896?

   A. Ohrbach   C. Straus
   B. Klein   D. Hoffman
              E. Bloomingdale
7. Adam Gimbel's first store was in

   A. Manhattan   C. White Plains, New York
   B. Brooklyn   D. Pennsylvania
              E. Vincennes, Indiana
8. What financier became chairman of the War Industries Board in World War I and chairman of the U.S. delegation to the United Nations Atomic Energy Commission right after World War II?

9. Which of these Wall Street firms are Jewish-based?
   A. Kuhn, Loeb   D. Lazard Frères
   B. Bache   E. Lehman Brothers
   C. Goldman, Sachs   F. Loeb, Rhoades
10. With which of them was the philanthropist Jacob Schiff associated?

The Jewish Initials Game (Business Division):

11. Jewish lawyer who helped found the world of Xerox and also made his mark in government service: S.L.
12. Came to America to work for the Rothschilds, changed his name from Schönberg, and became a fabulously wealthy financier; helped start the New York subways: A.B.
13. Headed a giant mail-order firm and started a foundation that dispensed millions for schools for black Americans: J.R.
14. Founder of the House of Rothschild (Do you know the full name?): M.A.R.
15. Polish-born Jew who built her American business empire so large that her name became nearly synonymous with her field, cosmetics: H.R.

Answers

1. Levi Strauss, who turned a cloth from Nîmes, France (*de Nîmes*), into trousers called denims, blue jeans, dungarees, or Levi's. 2. All but F. Zurich. 3. Started Filene's department store in Boston. 4. B. art to the Metropolitan Museum ($20 million worth). 5. Amoco. 6. C. Straus (Isidor and Nathan). 7. E. Vincennes, Indiana. 8. Bernard M. Baruch. 9. All but D. Lazard Frères. 10. A. Kuhn, Loeb. 11. Sol Linowitz. 12. August Belmont. 13. Julius Rosenwald, of Sears, Roebuck and Co. 14. Mayer Amschel Rothschild. 15. Helena Rubinstein.

66

—— "READ ALL ABOUT IT!" ——

It is *not* true that when a reporter has a hot story for a Yiddish-language newspaper he phones the city room and hollers: "Stop the presses! Remake the last page!" Nonetheless, here is a batch of questions about Jewish newspapers, publishers, and journalists.

1. The character called "Deep Throat" helped make this young Jewish journalist rich and famous. You have to name not only the real-life reporter but the actor who played him on the movie screen.
2. Name the major Israeli evening newspaper.
3. Israel's best-known English-language paper, also seen in the United States: _____.
4. During World War II, Joe Rosenthal, a Jewish photographer for the Associated Press, took a picture of some men on a mountaintop. The picture—one of the most famous of all time—won him a Pulitzer prize. Tell who the men were, what they were doing, and where.
5. What's the name of Abraham Cahan's Yiddish newspaper—the largest daily on New York's old East Side?
6. And what was the title of that paper's advice column?
7. If AP and UPI don't have it, chances are this news service will. It's an agency founded by a German Jew.
8. In the 1950s, Harry Golden became a household name with books of items collected from his small newspaper—a personal journal, really. Can you name the paper?
9. Around the turn of the century, a Jewish fellow from Tennessee built an ailing New York *Times* into a powerful institution. Who was he?
10. *Times* power later switched to the married-ins, whose family name is currently on top at the newspaper. What?
11. Who's the Jewish, stogie-puffing syndicated columnist who's been taking jabs at the Washington powerful for several administrations?

12. This Jewish journalist popularized the three-dot style and became a radio and TV fixture. Who was he?

13. The muckraker's muckraker, a Jew known as Izzy: _____.

14. What curmudgeonly Jewish-American newspaper cartoonist created the shmoo?

15. Charles MacArthur joined forces with a Jewish author to produce a play—later a movie—about the newspaper world. It's probably the most famous ever. Name it, and name the coauthor.

16. What does Roger Caras write about?

17. Name the identical-twin sisters who are competitors in the newspaper advice-column business.

18. Who was the Jewish gossip columnist who wrote from his "den"?

19. This newspaper publisher was half Jewish, a Hungarian immigrant. He led two major papers, the St. Louis *Post-Dispatch* and the New York *World*. He endowed Columbia University's prestigious School of Journalism. But he is best known for something else—something you hear about every year. What?

20. Walter Lippmann, the noted political columnist, editor, author, and government adviser, was associated first with *The New Republic* and the New York *World,* and then with which major newspaper, now defunct?

Answers

1. Carl Bernstein, played by Dustin Hoffman. 2. *Ma'arin.* 3. The Jerusalem *Post.* 4. They were U.S. marines, raising the flag at Iwo Jima. 5. *Forverts* (*Jewish Daily Forward*). 6. "Bintel Brief." 7. Reuters. 8. *The Carolina Israelite.* 9. Adolph S. Ochs. 10. Sulzberger. 11. Art Buchwald. 12. Walter Winchell. 13. I. F. Stone. 14. The same fellow who created Li'l Abner and pals: Al Capp (born Caplin). 15. *The Front Page;* Ben Hecht. 16. Pets and wildlife. 17. The Friedman sisters, Esther and Pauline, known as Ann Landers and Abigail "Dear Abby" Van Buren. 18. Leonard Lyons. 19. The Pulitzer prizes, which his will established (he's Joseph Pulitzer). 20. The New York *Herald Tribune.*

HAVE YOU HEARD
THIS ONE?

In a Broadway theater, just at the climax of an intense drama, a sudden cry is heard from the front row. A man clutches at his chest and falls out of his seat. The cry goes up: "A doctor! Get a doctor!"

A tall man in a dark suit rushes to the victim; the curtain is brought down and the ushers try vainly to quiet the crowd. Through it all, a woman's voice can be heard from the first mezzanine, hollering persistently, "Giff him chicken soup! Giff him some hot chicken soup!"

The doctor loosens the fallen man's tie and begins heart massage. Again the woman hollers from on high: "Oy, giff him a nice bowl chicken soup!"

The doctor continues massaging and pounding the man's chest as oxygen equipment is rushed down the aisle. "Giff him chicken soup!" the woman screams, until the doctor can bear it no longer.

"Lady!" he finally yells back. "This man is having a heart attack! Chicken soup can't help him!"

And the lady in the first mezzanine replies:

"——————————————!"

"Vell, it voodn't hoit!"

69

— JEWISH SPORTS —

Baseball, boxing, and a whole lot more. The questions cover but a tiny sampling of Jewish representation in the world of sports. There are no tough questions on statistics (such as what was Moe Berg's lifetime batting average?), but you need a very wide range of knowledge to do well.

1. Who was the left-handed pitching superstar who had his team's World Series assignment switched so he wouldn't be asked to pitch on Rosh Hashonah?
2. Horse racing's Triple Crown is made up of the Kentucky Derby, the Preakness, and a third race named for a Jewish financier. Name the race and the man.
3. What Jewish boxer held lightweight and welterweight titles for several years in the thirties?
4. And can you name the film made of his drug-plagued life?
5. More up to date, name the light-heavyweight champ of the seventies who wears a Star of David on his trunks and bills himself as "The Jewish Bomber"?
6. Hank Greenberg, the first Jew elected to baseball's Hall of Fame, hit fifty-eight home runs in 1938. For what team?
7. He may be the only sportscaster with a law degree, but that's not what makes him distinctive: it's his delivery and his demeanor. This Jewish self-proclaimed expert talked his way into being the best-known announcer of the seventies. Who?
8. From what two games did John M. Brunswick make millions?
9. Cleveland Indians slugging MVP third baseman of the early fifties, nickname "Flip": _____.
10. Swimmer Mark Spitz won four gold medals at the 1968 Olympics. How many did he win in 1972?
11. In 1909, Johnny Kling, the great Chicago Cubs catcher, took a year off from working on the diamond. What did he do instead?

12. Arnold "Red" Auerbach, coach of the dynastic Boston Celtics, was noted as a devotee of what instrument of oral gratification?

13. Fighter Max Schmeling's Jewish manager is credited with coining this loser's quotation: "We wuz robbed." Name the manager.

14. What pitcher saved the day for the Dodgers in the '59 World Series, winning two games and preserving the other two as relief ace?

15. The great Chicago Bears quarterback Sid Luckman, who led his team to four NFL championships, played first for an Ivy League college squad. Which?
    A. Brown   C. Yale
    B. Penn   D. Princeton
              E. Columbia

16. A Jewish boxer, Abe Attell, was world featherweight champ for more than a decade. Then, in 1919, he and gambling czar Arnold Rothstein were accused of fixing a major sports event. What event?

17. Which recent Yankee slugger was known as "The Kosher Bomber"?

18. He had one Jewish grandfather but wasn't raised a Jew himself; yet he wore a Star of David on his boxing trunks—a publicity gimmick, people said. He was the 1934–35 heavyweight champ. He had a kid brother, Buddy, who twice lost to Joe Louis. Who was he?

19. Name the international Jewish sports festival and tell how often it's been held of late.

20. What's Joey Cornblitt's sport?
    A. Basketball   C. Tennis
    B. Jai-alai   D. Soccer
              E. Boxing

Now match the Jewish athletes with the description:

21. Coached New York football Giants   Lillian Copeland
22. Light-heavyweight boxing champ,   Ruby Goldstein
    1916–20
23. Won discus gold medal in 1932   Dick Savitt
    Olympics
24. Left-handed pitcher   Abe Saperstein
25. Right-handed pitcher   Allie Sherman
26. Wimbledon champ, 1951   Nat Fleischer
27. Long-time boss of Harlem Globe-   Hirsch Jacobs
    trotters
28. Boxing writer   Battling Levinsky
29. Boxer turned referee   Moe Drabowsky
30. Trainer and breeder of horses   Bo Belinsky

Answers

1. Sandy Koufax. 2. Belmont Stakes, named for August Belmont. 3. Barney Ross (born Rosofsky). 4. *Monkey on My Back*. 5. Mike Rossman. 6. Detroit Tigers. 7. Of course: it's Howard ("The Mouth.") Cosell. 8. Billiards and bowling—he founded the Brunswick Corporation, which makes equipment for both. 9. Al Rosen. 10. An amazing seven. 11. He won the world professional billiards championship. 12. The cigar. 13. It was "Yussel the Muscle," Joe Jacobs, who also first pouted, "I shoulda stood in bed." 14. Larry Sherry. 15. E. Columbia. 16. The baseball World Series. (Bribes were said to have been paid to Chicago White Sox players to throw the first two games. The accusation was never proved.) 17. Ron Blomberg. 18. Max Baer. 19. Maccabiah; every four years. 20. B. Jai-alai. 21. Sherman. 22. Levinsky. 23. Copeland. 24. Belinsky. 25. Drabowsky. 26. Savitt. 27. Saperstein. 28. Fleischer. 29. Goldstein. 30. Jacobs.

—— AND THEN THERE WERE ——
THE BAD GUYS

A quick quiz on Jewish gangsters, criminals, thugs, and those accused of being same.

1. Who was the Jewish Very Important Criminal who, blessed by Dictator Batista, built up gambling in Cuba in the thirties?
2. A 1961 movie told the story of the *King of the Roaring Twenties*—this high-flying Jewish gambler. Name him.
3. Who was the high-powered racketeer—at the top of the national crime syndicate in the thirties—who was born Louis Buchalter?
4. Jacob Shapiro had an unusual nickname. What was it?
5. Name the Jewish gangster of the thirties with a reputation for his interest in women, his Hollywood partying (with George Raft and others), and his all-around toughness.
6. Of the five top gangsters you were just asked about in the first questions, four were executed by either the government or the underworld. Who managed to avoid a violent death?
7. Can you name the "enforcement" agency of the crime syndicate that was headed by Jews?
8. Who was Bobby Franks?
9. In 1951, Julius and Ethel Rosenberg were found guilty of conspiracy to commit wartime espionage. (Years later, the decision is still being questioned.) Convicted with them was Mrs. Rosenberg's brother. Name him.
10. Jack Ruby (*né* Rubenstein) gained eternal infamy by committing the first murder ever shown live on TV: the shooting of Lee Harvey Oswald. What was Ruby's occupation?

73

—— "HI! MY NAME'S IRVING. ——
WHAT'S YOURS?"

1. My name is Irving. I'm a songwriter. Even though I'm Jewish, two of my biggest hits are "White Christmas" and "Easter Parade." Who am I?
2. My name is Irving. I'm a songwriter also. I wrote "Swanee," "I Want to Be Happy," "Just a Gigolo," and a lot of other hits. But I'm best known for "Tea for Two." Who am I?
3. My name is Irving. I write books. So does my wife. So do my son and daughter. Well, not just books, actually—*best sellers*. My parents were named Wallechinsky. Who am I?
4. My name is Irving. I'm a correspondent for NBC-TV News. You've probably seen me on the evening newscast, standing in front of the White House. Who am I?
5. My name is Irving. I'm a movie and TV producer, but my biggest fame came because I was Jacqueline Susann's husband. Who am I?

—— WHAT'RE THEIR LINES? ——

Two quick matching tests on occupations of notable Jews. On the first five, if you recognize the names you should know the jobs.

1. Yossele Rosenblatt   mathematician
2. Tevye (in *Fiddler on the Roof*) historian
3. Boris Thomaschefsky   milkman
4. Barbara Tuchman   actor
5. Norbert Wiener   cantor

Now, for the second five, you're asked to match the notables to the work they did before they became famous, or on the side. To get these, you *really* have to know.

6. Billy Rose   wood chopper
7. Hillel   journalist
8. Spinoza   vintner
9. Rashi   stenographer
10. Theodor Herzl   lens polisher

Answers

1. Rosenblatt—cantor. 2. Tevye—milkman. 3. Thomaschefsky—actor. 4. Tuchman—historian. 5. Wiener—mathematician. 6. Rose—stenographer. 7. Hillel—wood chopper. 8. Spinoza—lens polisher. 9. Rashi—vintner. 10. Herzl—journalist.

—— WHO AND WHAT? ——

It takes a mind well versed in people and things Jewish to answer questions about who did what. Like who . . .

1. . . . was the only Jewish Miss America? (Bonus: What year?)
2. . . . launched the first atomic-powered submarine?
3. . . . is said to visit every Jewish home on Seder night?
4. . . . issued an order, as an army general, expelling traders and "the Jews as a clan" from an area of the United States?
5. . . . pioneered mass-produced housing and had towns named after them in New York and Pennsylvania?
6. . . . found the first Dead Sea Scrolls?
   - A. American archeologists
   - B. Jewish children at play
   - C. French musicians
   - D. Bedouins
   - E. Murderers hiding a body
7. . . . is often credited with creating the Hebrew calendar?
   - A. Hillel II
   - B. Maimonides
   - C. King David
   - D. King Saul
8. . . . destroyed the First Temple?
   - A. the Persians
   - B. the Romans
   - C. the Babylonians
   - D. barbarian hordes
   - E. renegade Jews
9. . . . was the only member of Anne Frank's family to survive?
10. . . . said, "I am that I am"?

Now match the deed with the doer.

11. Founded Reconstructionism in Judaism
12. Organized and edited the *Mishna*
13. Sparked community-health-care movement
14. Defended "the Chicago Seven"
15. Helped popularize Abstract Expressionist painting

Lillian Wald
William Kunstler
Mordecai Kaplan
Mark Rothko
Judah Ha-Nasi

76

The Jewish Initials Game. Who . . .

16. . . . composed the famous "Wedding March"?
    F_____ M_____

17. . . . made the girls swoon with "O My Papa" in the fifties?
    E_____ F_____

18. . . . was New York City Parks Commissioner and World's
    Fair chief?
    R_____ M_____

19. . . . led a revolt against the Romans that almost succeeded?
    B___ K_____

20. . . . founded the Hebrew University?
    C_____ W_____

21. . . . founded *The Reporter*?
    M___ A_____

22. . . . married Xavier Cugat?
    A_____ L_____

23. . . . organized the first Zionist Congress, in 1897?
    T_____ H_____

24. . . . was the chief Jewish supporter of the American Revo-
    lution?
    H_____ S_____

25. . . . sparked the revival of Hebrew?
    E_____ B___ Y_____

26. . . . worked as a ventriloquist with a puppet named Lamb-
    chop?
    S_____ L_____

27. . . . portrayed the character "Baby Snooks"?
    F_____ B_____

28. . . . built the empire known as CBS?
    W_____ P_____

29. . . . received and relayed wireless messages about the sink-
    ing of the *Titanic* (he later founded a broadcasting empire)?
    D_____ S_____

30. . . . cofounded the Spartacus Party and was murdered as a
    Communist revolutionary in Germany?
    R_____ L_____

——— WHERE? ———

This one is a quiz about places—streets, cities, countries, and various locations—that have a Jewish connection. You won't need a globe or a map to do well, just a smattering of Jewish Geography.

1. What do the names Baxter and Rivington have to do with Jews?
2. What's the most prominent institution in Liberty, New York?
3. And what's Kiamesha Lake known for?
4. What and where is Mea Shearim?
5. And what and where is the Marais?
6. Where can you find the Touro Synagogue?
7. Where have thousands of Jews stashed bits of paper with notes expressing hopes for the future?
8. Playwright S. N. Behrman's autobiography tells of growing up Jewish in what New England city?

9. In what city did Anne Frank and her family hide out from the Nazis? (Bonus: They hid in a warehouse/office on what canal?)

10. The stars were half Jewish on both sides. It was 1972 and Bobby Fischer (Jewish father) was taking on Boris Spassky (Jewish mother) for the world's chess title. Fischer won. In what capital city did this much-heralded event take place?

11. Are you old enough—and is your memory sharp enough—to recall "The Goldbergs" from radio and television? Well enough to know where Molly and her crew lived?

12. What's the large city nearest to Dachau, site of an early Nazi concentration camp?
    A. Frankfurt   C. Munich
    B. Berlin   D. Leipzig
          E. Warsaw

13. Where can you find Europe's oldest synagogue still in use?

14. Where did Golda Meir grow up?
    A. Jerusalem   C. Cracow
    B. Tel Aviv   D. New York
          E. Milwaukee

15. The main Jewish holidays are based on happenings in the Holy Land . . . except for Purim. Where did the story of Purim take place?

16. And can you name the capital city that figures prominently in the Purim story?

17. Sholem Aleichem did his greatest and final writing in New York, America. But in what country was he born?
    A. Turkey   C. Poland
    B. Germany   D. Russia
          E. U.S.A.

18. Where was Moses Maimonides born?
    A. Spain   C. Palestine
    B. Holland   D. England
          E. Egypt

19. With what city do you associate Arthur Fiedler?

20. Where is Stern College for Women?

21. And the Jewish Theological Seminary of America?

22. And Hebrew Union College?

23. And Brandeis University?
24. Name the island that was the major clearing house for immigrants to the U.S.A. from 1892 to 1943.
25. In which European capital can you find a popular Jewish restaurant called Bloom's?
26. In another capital of Europe, the best known Jewish dining spot is a deli called Goldenberg's. Where?
27. In this place, at one time, Jews made up less than 1 per cent of the population. Yet they accounted for some 17 per cent of the bankers, 16 per cent of the lawyers, and 10 per cent of the doctors. Then a disaster happened. Where and when?
28. What country is the birthplace of Reform Judaism?
    A. Russia   C. Canada
    B. United States   D. Portugal
           E. Germany
29. Probably the most famous Talmudic annotator of all time was Rashi, whose writings are still studied and revered nine centuries after he lived and worked. What was his homeland?
    A. France   C. Italy
    B. Poland   D. Transylvania
           E. Russia
30. In 1903, the British Government suggested a substitute for Palestine as a Jewish homeland. After much heated discussion, the idea was vetoed. Can you pick the place?
    A. Iran   C. New Zealand
    B. Uganda   D. Prince Edward Island

1. They're names of streets on New York's Lower East Side. 2. The Grossinger Hotel and Country Club, better known as Grossinger's, in the Catskills. 3. The Concord Hotel Resort. 4. It's the ultra-orthodox Jewish quarter of Jerusalem. 5. The section of Paris that includes that city's Jewish quarter. 6. Newport, Rhode Island. 7. In cracks in the Western Wall. 8. Worcester, Massachusetts (*The Worcester Account*). 9. Amsterdam. (Bonus: the Prinsengracht Canal; the building is today maintained as a memorial.) 10. Reykjavik, Iceland. 11. The Bronx (across the way from Mrs. Bloom). 12. C. Munich. 13. In Prague—the Old-New Synagogue, dating at least to the fourteenth century. (The nearby Pinkas Synagogue is even older but no longer serves for worship; it's a memorial of the Nazi killings.) 14. E. Milwaukee. (She graduated from North Division High School, there, in 1916.) 15. Persia. 16. Shushan. 17. D. Russia. 18. A. Spain. 19. Boston (long-time leader of the Boston "Pops" Orchestra). 20. New York City. (It's a division of Yeshiva University.) 21. Also New York City. 22. Cincinnati. 23. Waltham, Massachusetts. 24. Ellis Island. 25. London. 26. Paris. 27. Germany, just before the Holocaust. 28. E. Germany. 29. A. France. 30. B. Uganda.

HAVE YOU HEARD
THIS ONE?

Moskowitz eats lunch at Goldstein's Deli, in the Garment Center . . . not occasionally but every weekday for thirty-seven years. And every day—for thirty-seven years—barley soup. He doesn't even need to order. Goldstein sees through the window that Moskowitz is coming, he puts a bowl of barley soup on the counter.

On this particular day, everything begins as it has for thirty-seven years. Moskowitz comes in, Goldstein has the soup waiting. Moskowitz sits.

"Hey, Goldstein!" bellows Moskowitz. "Taste this soup!"

"What's the matter?" asks Goldstein.

"Just taste!"

"What are you talking? You always like my barley soup. Thirty-seven years you like my barley soup!"

"Taste!"

"What? Do you have kishkeh for a brain? Have you ever *not* liked my barley soup?"

"Taste!"

"Okay, to shut you up. . . . Where's the spoon?"

"————!"

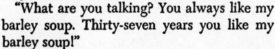

"Aha!"

—— WHEN? ——

Jews traditionally date happenings relative to major events in their lives. "When did we move to Philadelphia? Let's see. It was the year after my Aunt Chasha died, in the same month as little Heshie's bar mitzvah. . . ." These questions test *your* knowledge of what happened when.

1. What year was the Warsaw Ghetto uprising?
2. Roughly when would you place the start of Reform Judaism?
   A. early 1800s   C. early 1900s
   B. late 1800s   D. middle 1900s
3. In fourteen hundred ninety-two, Columbus sailed the ocean blue. But what happened to the Spanish Jews in that year?
4. In 1949–50, Operation Magic Carpet transferred what kind of Jews to Israel?
5. When was the first Jewish community established in the U.S.A.?
   A. 1621   C. 1777
   B. 1654   D. 1810

Answers

1. 1943. 2. A. early 1800s. 3. They were expelled from their country by King Ferdinand. 4. Yemenite. 5. B. 1654 (in what later became New York City).

83

—— WHY? ——

Is there a better question than "Why?" So here are five "Whys" for you to ponder.

1. Jews at Purim sometimes write the name of Haman on the soles of their shoes. Why?
2. "May all your teeth fall out except one" is a popular old Jewish curse. Why "except one"?
3. It's very important for Orthodox Jews to bring a handkerchief to a wedding. Why?
4. Poland and Lithuania had large concentrations of Jews during and after the Middle Ages. Why?
5. It is often argued that the Ten Commandments are really only nine. Why?

Answers

1. So that, by walking, they can obliterate the name of the holiday's villain. 2. So that "in that one may you have a permanent toothache." 3. So that, even though prohibited from touching someone of the opposite sex, they may dance, each partner holding an end of the cloth. 4. Because they remained pagan long after other countries in Europe, so their kings, having no religion to force upon the countries, allowed the Jews to be. 5. Because the first is really a statement, not a command: "I am the Lord thy God, who brought thee out of the land of Egypt, out of the house of bondage."

84

"HI! MY NAME'S ISAAC. — WHAT'S YOURS?

1. My name is Isaac. I write Yiddish stories about shtetls, with mystical overtones. Translated into English, my works are very popular in America, where I live. I usually go by three names. Who am I?
2. My name is Isaac. I played the violin as a youngster, like a lot of other Jewish boys in America. But I made my concert debut at eleven and went on to musical fame. Who am I?
3. My name is Isaac. I also write—about everything from Shakespeare to bawdy limericks, with a heavy dose of science and science fiction thrown in. I almost can't count the number of books I've produced—I guess it's around two hundred. They say I'm more than prolific—I'm an obsessive writer. Who am I?
4. My name is Isaac. (I use the Hebrew form.) I'm an Israeli. I commanded the Israeli Army during the Six-day War. Later I was made ambassador to the U.S.A. and served my country as prime minister. Who am I?
5. My name is Isaac. You can see my full name in your favorite delicatessen; just look at a salami. Who am I?

Answers

1. Isaac Bashevis Singer. 2. Isaac Stern. 3. Isaac Asimov. 4. Yitzchak Rabin. 5. Isaac Gellis.

85

—— COUNTING HEADS ——

Here are ten questions on Jewish population statistics from around the world. Even a vague knowledge of Where the Jews Are will help.

1. The Jewish population of the world today is estimated at:
   A. 2.5 million   C. 14.5 million
   B. 6.5 million   D. 22 million
            E. 38 million
2. Are there now more Jews world-wide than just before World War II or fewer?
3. American Jews make up ____ of world Jewry.
   A. 5 per cent   C. 40 per cent
   B. 25 per cent   D. 80 per cent
            E. 90 per cent
4. Roughly how many Jews are there in Canada?
   A. 5,000   C. 300,000
   B. 50,000   D. 750,000
            E. 2,000,000
5. About how many synagogues are there in the U.S.A.?
   A. 1,000   C. 3,000
   B. 1,500   D. 7,000
            E. 25,000
6. New York City has more Jewish people than any other city in the world—roughly 1.25 million, with another million in the metropolitan area. Which of these cities and metropolitan regions have more than 100,000 Jews?

A. Boston
B. Chicago
C. Los Angeles
D. Miami
E. Philadelphia
F. Washington
G. Buenos Aires
H. Haifa
I. Jerusalem

J. Kiev
K. Leningrad
L. London
M. Montreal
N. Moscow
O. Odessa
P. Paris
Q. Ramat Gan
R. Tel Aviv

S. Toronto

Match these countries with their approximate Jewish populations:

7. Germany   120,000
8. France   2,700,000
9. Soviet Union   550,000
10. Republic of South Africa   32,000

Answers

1. C. 14.5 million. 2. Still fewer. (There were an estimated 16.7 million before the war.) 3. C. 40 per cent (5.8 million). 4. C. 300,000. 5. C. 3,000. 6. All of them. 7. Germany—32,000. 8. France—550,000. 9. Soviet Union—2,700,000. 10. Republic of South Africa—120,000.

Depending on where their ancestors came from, or who they were, Jews fit into various groupings. Some of the dividing lines are so sharp that to cross them in marriage has traditionally been considered, at the least, a bold move. These questions cover just some of the splits.

1. Among ancient Jews, the Kohanim were the priests. Who were the Levites?
2. And what's the name for the third great ancient division—including everyone else?
3. Two broad divisions among Jews are Sephardim and Ashkenazim. Which group comes from Central and Eastern Europe?
4. Which spent much of their history as near-nobility?
5. World-wide, one group outnumbers the other about thirteen to one. Which?
6. Among many Ashkenazic Jews in America one frequently hears talk of what sounds like two battling armies from Eastern Europe, the L_____ and the G_____.
7. Cochin Jews and Bene Israel Jews both trace their ancestry to _____.
8. For which group of Jews is dance a form of prayer?
9. The Falashas are a tribe of black Jews claiming descent from the tribe of Levi. With which country do you associate them?
10. Who were the Marranos?

Answers

1. They were caretakers of the Temple, as well as learned judges and teachers and helpers of the priests. 2. Israelites. 3. The Ashkenazim. 4. The Sephardim. 5. The Ashkenazim. 6. Litvaks and Galitzianer (those from Lithuania and Galicia). 7. India. 8. The Chasidim. 9. Ethiopia. 10. Spanish and Portuguese Jews who converted to Christianity under force but continued Jewish practices in secret.

—— THE STATE OF ISRAEL ——

The modern Jewish nation attracts interest for political, social, cultural, religious, and emotional reasons. So whether you've been there or not, you've probably learned a few things about the country. Test yourself.

1. The State of Israel was proclaimed in 1948. What was the exact date?
2. What's the name of Israel's biggest airport?
3. What's on the Israeli flag besides a blue Star of David?
4. Tel Aviv and Jerusalem are the largest cities in the country. What's the third largest?
5. True or false: Israel is on the metric system.
6. Which countries border on Israel?
   A. Lebanon   C. Jordan
   B. Syria   D. Iraq
             E. Egypt
7. In 1976, Israeli commandos daringly rescued a planeful of hostages from Arab skyjackers at Entebbe, Uganda. The airline was *not* El Al, the Israeli fleet. So, what was it?
8. What's the difference between a kibbutz and a moshav?
9. Roughly how much of the Israeli population lives on kibbutzim?
   A. less than 5 per cent   C. about half
   B. about a third   D. about 90 per cent
10. What is the Israeli Parliament called?
11. The letter of encouragement to the Zionist cause written by the British Foreign Secretary in 1917 is known to historians as . . . ?
12. Who was Israel's first prime minister? its first president?
13. What's Mogen David Adom?
14. What's the major industry of Israel?
    A. Citrus fruit   C. Tires
    B. Diamond finishing   D. Frozen foods
15. What's Arkia?
16. Name the famous American gangster who took up residence

in Israel in 1972 to avoid prosecution for income-tax evasion
at home.
17. What was Golda's name before it was Meir?
18. What was James McDonald in the history of Israel?
19. How long after the Proclamation of Independence before the
Arab attack that signaled the War of Liberation?
20. How many official languages does Israel have?

Answers

1. May 14, 1948. 2. Ben Gurion (formerly called Lod International). 3. Two broad horizontal stripes. 4. Haifa. 5. True. 6. All
but *D*. Iraq 7. Air France. 8. A kibbutz is a thoroughly communal
farm, a moshav is a community with private property in which only
some economic functions are pooled. 9. *A*. Less than 5 per cent. 10.
Knesset. 11. The Balfour Declaration. 12. David Ben Gurion;
Chaim Weizmann. 13. The Israeli version of the Red Cross. 14. *B*.
Diamond finishing. 15. The Israeli domestic airline. 16. Meyer
Lansky. 17. Myerson. 18. First U.S. ambassador to the new country. 19. One day. 20. Two: Hebrew and Arabic.

DID YOU EVER
—— STOP TO THINK . . . ? ——

. . . which eye Moshe Dayan's patch is on?

Answer

It's the left.

—— THE LAST LETTER ——

Here's a difficult matching problem. The descriptions at left can each be satisfied by a word starting with "Z," to be found in the list on the right.

1. Chief written work of Kabbalah, the Jewish mystical doctrine of the universe.
2. Leah's handmaid, in the Book of Genesis.
3. Moses killed an Egyptian guard and fled to Midian, where he married her.
4. Controlled Paramount Pictures for some forty years. First name Adolph.
5. Showman Flo, creator of the "Follies."
6. Marx Brother No. 4.
7. Creator of Esperanto, an artificial "international language."
8. Jewish actor Paul Muni played the screen role of this non-Jewish writer who went to prison for defending a Jew.
9. Jewish-born Boris Pasternak created this doctor.
10. Russian-born violinist of note, father of American actor.

Zola

Zamenhof

Zilpah

Zohar

Zhivago

Zukor

Zimbalist

Zipporah

Zeppo

Ziegfeld

Answers

1. Zohar. 2. Zilpah. 3. Zipporah. 4. Zukor. 5. Ziegfeld. 6. Zeppo. 7. Zamenhof. 8. Zola. 9. Zhivago. 10. Zimbalist.

— THE MATCH GAME —

Can you figure out the marriages reported here?

1. A non-Jewish king marries a Jewess, soon to be a heroine to her people.

2. A Jewish gambler marries a famous Jewish pop singer.

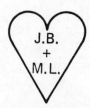

3. Benny Kubelsky marries Sadie Marks. For decades they come into America's living rooms via radio and TV.

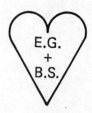

4. An actor and his co-star, playing Yetta Marmelstein, take the plunge.

5. He married—among others— Ava Gardner and Lana Turner. He was a clarinet player who was born Abraham Isaac Arshawsky, but he was better known as ————.

HAVE YOU HEARD THIS ONE?

God finishes composing his Commandments. Off he goes to the leader of the Egyptians. "You want some of my Commandments?" he asks the Pharaoh.

"What kind of commandments?" asks the Egyptian.

"Oh, 'Thou shalt not steal,' 'Thou shalt not commit adultery,' stuff like that," says God.

"Forget it," says Pharaoh.

God goes to the head Babylonian. Same thing: no takers. So he goes to Moses. Moses doesn't even ask what kind of commandments he's offering. He gets right to the point: "How much do they cost?"

"Gornisht," says God. "Nothing. They're free."

Says Moses: "_____
____!"

"Swell! In that case, we'll take ten!"

——— NUMBERS ———

These questions all deal with one number or another. But don't panic: you don't need any special math ability, just a wide variety of Jewish knowledge.

1. If you received thirty-six dollars from a person steeped in Jewishness, you would know immediately the significance of the gift. Which is . . . ?
2. How old was Sarah when the angels told her she and Abraham would have a child?
3. With whom do you associate the number 186,000?
4. Lag b'Omer is the ——— day of the counting of the Omer.
   A. thirty-third   C. fourth
   B. fifth   D. twentieth
5. Traditional Jewish blessing for long life: "You should live until ————."
6. How many Hebrew words in the Shema?
7. How many divine commandments in the Torah?
   A. 10   C. 100
   B. 77   D. 613
8. How many years did the Exodus take?
9. And how many days and nights was Moses on Mount Sinai?
10. How many Jews came to America on the Mayflower?

Answers

1. That the amount is twice *chai*, the number eighteen and the Jewish symbol for life. 2. Ninety. 3. Albert Michelson, the Jewish physicist who measured the speed of light as 186,000 miles per second, winning him the Nobel Prize for Physics in 1907. 4. A. Thirty-third. 5. 120. 6. Six. 7. D. 613. 8. Forty. 9. Forty. 10. Zero.

94

— JEWISH MATH TEST —

Take the number of days the War of 1967 lasted: _____. Multiply by the number of questions asked at Passover: _____. Add the number of plagues: _____. Subtract the number of days of Shiva: _____. Divide by the number of spaces for candles on a Chanukah menorah: _____.

What do you get? _____.

Answers

6 days times 4 questions plus 10 plagues minus 7 days divided by 9 candles equals . . . 3.

— JEWISH MATH TEST, —
GRADUATE LEVEL

Take the number in a minyan: _____. Multiply by the number of times *tefillin* are wound around the arm: _____. Divide by the number of daughters Tevye has in *Fiddler on the Roof*: _____. Add the number of zuzim paid for Chad Gadya in the Passover song: _____. Subtract the date of Tu b'Shevat, the Jewish Arbor Day: _____.

Total: _____.

Answer

10 male adult Jews times 7 times around divided by 5 daughters plus 2 zuzim minus the 15th day of Shevat equals . . . 1.

—— ONE LITTLE WORD ——

The answer to each question here is a single word—sometimes English, sometimes Yiddish, sometimes Hebrew. Try.

1. What's the adverb that goes with kosher and means really, very, strictly kosher?
2. And what's the name for the fringes at the ends of a tallit?
3. What is it that Jews sell to a non-Jew once a year and then buy back a week later?
4. What are Jewish children encouraged to steal for ransom?
5. According to the legend, of what material was the golem made?
6. What's the better-known name of the Women's Zionist Organization of America?
7. To some, Norman Podhoretz is known for his book *Making It*. But he's better known as editor of the Jewish intellectual's monthly pride and joy, the magazine called _____.
8. What's the word for the side curls worn by Chasidim?
9. Shomrim is the name of a society of Jewish _____ in New York City.
10. It's a Hebrew word, commonly used by Christians and Moslems in prayer. What's the word?
11. Give another name for the Sephardic tongue usually called Ladino.
12. George Eliot created a book about a Jewish character named Daniel _____.
13. Which country is the Jewish capital of South America?
14. Chemical element 99 is named for a Jewish physicist. Name that element.
15. Mobster Mickey Cohen's state: _____.

tina. 14. Einsteinium. 15. California.
Policemen. 10. Amen. 11. Judesmo. 12. Deronda. 13. Argen-
Clay. 6. Hadassah. 7. *Commentary.* 8. Peyot (or payess). 9.
Passover). 4. Afikoman (an assigned piece of Passover matzoh). 5.
1. Glatt. 2. Tzitzit. 3. Chometz (leavened food, not allowed on

—— TRUE OR FALSE? ——

It takes only one word to answer these twenty questions also,
and the choices here are simpler: the answer is either True or
False. Decide which and circle the proper letter.

T F 1. In days past, the title Rabbi was often conferred on
        unordained men.

T F 2. There are no synagogues in Moscow.

T F 3. "Did Your Mother Come From Ireland?" was com-
        posed by a Jew.

T F 4. The bar mitzvah ceremony dates back to the time of
        the Second Temple

T F 5. In post Biblical times, Jews have never allowed polyg-
        amy.

T F 6. *The Last Angry Man* is about a Jewish defense at-
        torney.

T F 7. The Dead Sea Scrolls have been identified as writ-
        ings of members of a Jewish sect from about the time
        of Jesus.

T F 8. Jews were the first people to practice circumcision.

T F 9. According to the Mishna, "A learned bastard takes
        precedence over an uneducated High Priest."

T F 10. Wearing tefillin is one of the most important rituals
        of the Sabbath.

T F 11. The term Zionism, concerning the movement to re-
        turn Israel to the Jewish people, was coined in the
        seventeenth century.

97

T F 12. Haifa is south of Tel Aviv.

T F 13. Chelm does not exist.

T F 14. Jews in Europe were accused of causing the plague known as the Black Death in the fourteenth century, resulting in pogroms.

T F 15. According to Jewish practice, when a Torah reader misreads a word, the congregation is obliged to correct him mentally but say nothing, for fear of humiliating him before God.

T F 16. The Western Wall (the Wailing Wall) is a remnant of the First Temple at Jerusalem.

T F 17. According to the Bible, the Lord ordered his children not only not to eat pork but not to touch the dead carcass of a pig.

T F 18. Shemini Atzeret is the day after Simchat Torah.

T F 19. Luis de Torres, a Jewish interpreter with Christopher Columbus in 1492, is credited with bringing back and introducing to Europe tobacco and turkeys.

T F 20. The basic formation of the hora is a figure eight.

Answers

1. True. 2. False. 3. True—Dublin-reared Michael Carr (born Cohen) did the job. 4. False—only to the fourteenth century. 5. False—here and there it has been accepted, where Jews have lived among people who practice it. 6. False—it's about a Jewish physician, Dr. Sam Abelman. 7. True. 8. False—ancient Egyptians and many other cultures did it earlier. 9. True. 10. False—tefillin are not worn on the Sabbath. 11. False—the term is less than one hundred years old. 12. False—it's north. 13. False—although it is the setting of many "dumb" jokes, it is in fact a town in Poland. 14. True. 15. False—congregants are expected to shout the correction, and the reader must reread the passage. 16. False—it's the last standing part of the Second Temple. 17. True—see Deuteronomy 14:8. 18. False—it's the day before. 19. True. 20. False—a circle.

—— PRAYER ——

These are fairly elementary questions on prayer in the practice of Judaism.

1. What's the Yiddish word for pray?
2. Hamotzi is the common name for a prayer said every day. What is it?
3. What's the word for swaying back and forth during prayer?
4. The morning service begins with _____.
5. The most famous prayer of the holiest Jewish day is not in Hebrew. Can you name the holiday, the prayer, and the language?
6. That prayer is chanted three times. Is it done progressively louder or progressively softer?
7. Does Jewish law insist that public prayer be held in a synagogue?
8. Is the Amidah recited silently, softly, or loudly?
9. What does Kaddish say about death?
10. What does a praying Jew do during the Shemoneh Esreh?
11. And while chanting the words "anachnu korim"?
12. What's the traditional deathbed prayer of Jews?
13. At what time of day is Modeh Ani recited?
14. Which comes first, Ma'ariv or Mincha?
15. What Ashkenazic practice is widely associated with the Yizkor service?

Answers

——— THE BIBLE ———

Match the biblical character with the appropriate quality:

1. Solomon   patience
2. Job   hospitality
3. Samson   courage
4. David   strength
5. Abraham   wisdom

6. Who was the first baby born on earth?
7. How did Jonah end up in the sea? Did he fall or jump, or was he thrown in (and if so, by whom)?
8. Why did Jacob and his children leave home and go to Egypt?
    A. to seek an audience with Pharaoh
    B. to escape a famine
    C. to live with Jacob's wife
    D. to be near the great Egyptian university
    E. to start a matzoh factory
9. Who interpreted "MENE, MENE, TEKEL, UPHARSIN," the handwriting on the wall? (Bonus: What did it mean?)
10. Who wrote the Book of Proverbs?
    A. David   C. Solomon
    B. Moses   D. Jesse
        E. Isaiah

11. The Shema, the central prayer of Judaism, derives from which book of the Bible?
12. God's test for Abraham was the order to sacrifice his son. First, name the son. Second, tell the method of sacrifice planned.
13. What biblical character was from the land of Uz?
14. In which book is it said, "For the living know that they shall die; but the dead know not anything . . ."?
15. What was the weather like the day God gave Moses the Ten Commandments?

    A. sunny   C. thundering and lightning
    B. rainy   D. the Bible does not say

16. What relationship was Aaron to Moses?
17. Only two animals speak in the Bible: the serpent, who talks to Eve, is one. What's the other?
18. According to the Bible, the Messiah would be descended from what great leader?

Match the biblical character with the statement that fits:

19. Found the infant Moses in the river   Miriam
20. Brought water from a stone   Solomon
21. David's most celebrated child   Moses
22. Punished with leprosy for speaking   Pharaoh's daughter
    against Moses

Name at least eight of the twelve Minor Prophets. For a help, the first initials of their names are given:

23. _____	H	N
24. _____	J	H
25. _____	A	Z
26. _____	O	H
27. _____	M	M
28. _____	J	Z
29. _____		
30. _____		

1. Solomon—wisdom. 2. Job—patience. 3. Samson—strength. 4. David—courage. 5. Abraham—hospitality. 6. Cain. 7. The crew threw him in. 8. B. to escape a famine. 9. Daniel. (Bonus: Balshazzar, the Babylonian king, was doomed to lose his kingdom—See Daniel 5.) 10. C. Solomon. 11. Deuteronomy (6:4). 12. Isaac; murder by knife. 13. Job. 14. Ecclesiastes (9:5). 15. C. Thunder-ing and lightning. 16. His brother. 17. Balaam's ass, who complains of being beaten. 18. King David. 19. Pharaoh's daughter. 20. Moses. 21. Solomon. 22. Miriam. 23–30. Eight chosen from the twelve: Hosea, Joel, Amos, Obadiah, Jonah, Micah, Nahum, Habakkuk, Zephaniah, Haggai, Zechariah, Malachi.

—— A BIBLICAL MINI-WORD FIND ——

Here's a tiny Word Find containing just thirteen three-letter words found in the Bible. They're written every which way.

```
N H D E V E
J O B E F L
G R D A N I
Z Z A S S C
B U Z L O T
M A H W N R
```

Answers

HORIZONTAL: EVE, JOB, ASS, BUZ, LOT VERTICAL: HOR, SON, ELI DIAGONAL: NOD, GOD, DEN, HUZ, COW

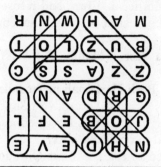

—— HOLIDAYS AND FESTIVALS ——

Jewish holidays come in all manner and form. So do these questions.

1. On what holiday do the pious cast crumbs from their pockets into water?
2. Shavuot celebrates
   A. the harvest and the giving of the law.
   B. the rebuilding of the Temple.
   C. the Exodus of the Jews from Egypt.
   D. the birth of a prophet.
3. And what does Simchat Torah celebrate?
4. Lag b'Omer is
   A. a happy day in the midst of a sad period.
   B. a sad day in the midst of a happy period.
   C. the happiest day of a happy period.
   D. the saddest day of a sad period.
   E. a fast day.

5. What color is an etrog?
6. Oh, once there was a wicked, wicked man. What was his name?
7. Why did he want to murder all the Jews?
    A. Because his Jewish wife ran off with another man.
    B. Because Mordecai, a Jew, had refused to bow to him.
    C. Because he feared a Jewish takeover of his government.
    D. Because a seer told him the stars wanted Jews destroyed.
8. The first day of Rosh Hashonah never falls on
    A. Saturday   C. Saturday or Sunday
    B. Sunday   D. Sunday, Wednesday, or Friday
9. What food is eaten on Tisha b'Av?
10. Who is supposed to ask the Four Questions at the Passover Seder?
11. Which holiday has been associated with planting trees in Israel?
12. Shemini Atzeret and Simchat Torah come at the end of which seven-day festival?
13. How many corners to hamantaschen?
14. Who lit the eternal lamp in the Temple—the light that miraculously burned for eight days?
15. Charoset, that favorite Passover dish, is a delicious mixture of apples, chopped nuts, cinnamon, honey, and wine. What does it represent?
16. What does the ram's horn (shofar) recall from the Bible?
17. The lulav, a symbol of Succot, is a palm branch to which are attached pieces of
    A. willow.   C. willow and myrtle.
    B. myrtle.   D. willow and pine.
                    E. just pine.
18. What four letters are on the sides of a dreydl?
19. Which day is referred to as "the Sabbath of Sabbaths"?
20. What's tekiah gedolah?

Match the festivals with the Hebrew dates:

21. Passover   10th of Tishri
22. Yom Kippur   25th of Kislev
23. Purim   15th of Tishri
24. Chanukah   14th of Adar
25. Succot   15th of Nisan

And now match the important days with the foods:

26. Chanukah   blintzes
27. Shavuot   latkes
28. Sabbath   macaroons
29. Passover   honey cake
30. Rosh Hashonah   challah

Answers

1. Rosh Hashonah. 2. A. the harvest and the giving of the law. 3. The conclusion of the yearly cycle of Torah reading and the start once again. 4. A. a happy day in the midst of a sad period. 5. Yellow. 6. Haman was his name, sir. 7. B. Because Mordecai, a Jew, had refused to bow to him. 8. D. Sunday, Wednesday, or Friday. 9. None—it's a fast day. 10. The youngest male child present who is able. 11. Hamishah Asar b'Shevat (Tu b'Shevat). 12. Succot. 13. Three. 14. Judah the Maccabee. 15. The clay formed into bricks by Jews in slavery in Egypt. 16. The ram Abraham was allowed to sacrifice in place of his son, Isaac. 17. C. willow and myrtle. 18. Gimel, shin, nun, hei (spelling Goshnah, to Goshen, the place to which Jacob sent Judah, or, in different order, spelling an acronym for the Hebrew sentence "A great miracle happened there"). 19. Yom Kippur. 20. The last shofar call, a very long blast. 21. 15th of Nisan. 22. 10th of Tishri. 23. 14th of Adar. 24. 25th of Kislev. 25. 15th of Tishri. 26. Latkes. 27. Blintzes. 28. Challah. 29. Macaroons. 30. Honey cake.

— MIXED-UP MENU —

Here's part of a holiday menu, with each food item scrambled. Unscramble the list and the circled letters will spell out the special occasion.

1. SRALYEP = ⊙ _ _ _ _ _ _

2. KNEABONSH = _ _ _ _ _ _ _ _ ⊙

3. TEDGERS GOA = _ _ _ ⊙ _ _ _ _ _ _

4. WATT LASER = _ ⊙ _ _ _ _ _ _ _

5. ESTROACH = ⊙ _ _ _ _ _ _ _

6. ROSEISHARDH = ⊙ _ _ _ _ _ _ _ _ _

7. HOTZAM = ⊙ _ _ _ _ _

8. NEWI = _ _ _ ⊙

9. ADYNKHALC = _ _ ⊙ _ _ ⊙ _ _ _

10. The special occasion: ⊙⊙⊙⊙⊙ ⊙⊙⊙⊙

Answers

1. PARSLEY. 2. SHANKBONE. 3. ROASTED EGG. 4. SALT WATER. 5. CHAROSET. 6. HORSERADISH. 7. MATZOH. 8. WINE. 9. KNAYDLACH. 10. PESACH MEAL.

106

—— DID YOU EVER STOP ——
TO FIGURE . . . ?

. . . how many candles are needed for the entire Chanukah celebration?

Answer

Start with one and add one for each succeeding day, plus an extra each day for the shammes, the one used to light the others. So, two the first day, three the second day, four the third day, five the fourth day, six the fifth day, seven the sixth day, eight the seventh day, nine the eighth day. That's 2+3+4+5+6+7+8+9=44. Or as the mathematicians would put it, $\frac{8(2+9)}{2}$.

—— THE TEN PLAGUES ——

At the Passover Seder, participants pour ten drops of wine from their cups to symbolize the ten plagues visited upon the Egyptians. Here's a list of the ten . . . plus an extra curse that *wasn't* among the Egyptians' headaches. Can you pick out the problem that's out of place?

A. Blood
B. Frogs
C. Famine
D. Vermin
E. Wild beasts

F. Murrain
G. Boils
H. Hail
I. Locusts
J. Darkness

K. The slaying of the first-born

C. Famine doesn't belong. (They had enough troubles.)

—— SCRAMBLED CALENDAR ——

A friend gives you a beautiful new Hebrew calendar. Beautiful, but the glue is no good. The calendar falls apart and the pages fly in the wind. When you finally gather them all, you need to put them back into the proper order—beginning with the first month of the Jewish year. Can you do it? The last two are marked for you.

_____	Nisan	_____	Cheshvan
_____	Kislev	_____	Tevet
_____	Tishri	11	Av
_____	Tammuz	_____	Adar
_____	Iyar	12	Elul
_____	Sivan	_____	Shevat

1. Tishri. 2. Cheshvan. 3. Kislev. 4. Tevet. 5. Shevat. 6. Adar. 7. Nisan. 8. Iyar. 9. Sivan. 10. Tammuz.

—— CUSTOMS AND PRACTICES ——

Fifteen questions on Jewish practices hundreds (or thousands) of years old.

1. What's one sound you can be pretty sure of hearing at a brit milah (or bris)?
2. What's broken during a Jewish wedding ceremony? By whom? How?
3. What's inside tefillin?
4. And what's in a mezuzah?
5. What does bar mitzvah mean?
6. No shoes. No sex. No shave. No haircut. No cosmetics. No new clothes. No work. Sit on the floor, or on a low stool. What do all these add up to?
7. A pious male Jew is buried with what article of religious paraphernalia?
8. Explain the difference in baby-naming practices of the Ashkenazim and the Sephardim.
9. In the orthodox wedding ceremony, the bride walks _____ times around her groom.
10. On her wedding day, the traditional orthodox bride does something to ensure that she will not distract her man from study. What?
11. If a man tells you he is going to celebrate a pidyon ha-ben, what can you logically deduce?
    A. He is about to be married.
    B. His mother or father has died.
    C. He and his wife have had their first child.
    D. He and his wife have had their first child—a son.
    E. Either his son is bar mitzvah or his daughter bat mitzvah.
12. Jewish practice calls for visitors to do what with their hands after leaving a cemetery?

A. wring them

B. wash them

C. raise them in the air

D. cover them briefly with dirt

E. fold them and say a prayer for continued life

13. The Mogen David, the six-pointed star, is not only the official emblem of the State of Israel—it is the accepted symbol of the Jewish people. But its use is a recent development. In the Middle Ages, another ornament was considered the chief Jewish symbol. What was that?

14. For how long do observant Jews recite kaddish after the death of a parent?

A. seven days   C. ninety days

B. thirty days   D. eleven months

E. twelve months

15. If you see a woman remove a man's shoe, spit on the ground, and say, "Thus shall be done to the man who will not build his brother's house," what's going on?

Answers

1. A baby crying. (Wouldn't you?) 2. A glass, by the groom, who steps on it. 3. Quotations from Deuteronomy (6:4–9 and 11:13–21) and Exodus (13:1–16). 4. The same words from Deuteronomy. 5. Son of the commandment. 6. Shivah, the seven-day mourning period. 7. His tallit. 8. Ashkenazic custom dictates that a child be named after someone dead; Sephardic custom is to take the name of a living relative. 9. Seven (usually). 10. Shaves her head. 11. D. . . first child—a son. 12. B. wash them. 13. The menorah. 14. D. eleven months. 15. A chalitza ceremony. According to Jewish law, when a married man dies childless, his unmarried brother is obliged to marry the widow. She, however, may marry another of her own choosing if he agrees to the ceremony called chalitza.

HAVE YOU HEARD
THIS ONE?

Mrs. Feinberg takes a seat next to another
Jewish lady on the New York-to-Miami flight.
They're not even off the ground when Mrs. F.
notices the other's diamond ring—a rock that
resembles a sparkling golf ball.

"My, my, vot a gorgeous rink," says Mrs.
Feinberg.

"Denk you," says the lady.

"By me, dot looks almost as big like the
Star from Efrica," says Mrs. F.

"Vell," says the lady, "ectually, dis is
nomber two in de voild, right *after* the Star
from Efrica."

"Is dot a fect? You must be very heppy."

"Vell, it ain't such a joy mit a rink like dis.
It comes mit dis diamond, unfortunately, de
Lipschitz curse, vot never leafs you as lonk as
you is vearink dis rink."

"Oh, mine Gott! Vot's dat?"

"————————————!"

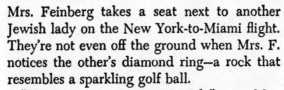

"Lipschitz!"

—— MISHPOCHEH ——

You probably have enough trouble keeping track of who's who in your own family, but let's see what you know about a few famous Jewish relatives.

1. How were Ruth and Naomi, of Bible fame, related?
2. Bel Kaufman, who wrote *Up the Down Staircase*—who was her famous grandfather?
3. What famous Jewish concert pianist had an even more famous non-Jewish father-in-law?
4. Another man important in his own right was Lazar Moiseyevich Kaganovich, a key Russian official for many years. He, too, had a non-Jewish in-law who was even more famous. Any idea who?
5. What was the name of Shylock's daughter?
   A. Rachel   C. Jessica
   B. Rebecca   D. Judith
              E. Miriam

Answers

1. Naomi was Ruth's mother-in-law.   2. Sholem Aleichem.   3. Vladimir Horowitz, son-in-law of Toscanini.   4. Joseph Stalin, his brother-in-law.   5. C. Jessica.

—— FILL IN THE BLANKS ——

Key words are missing here from five well-known expressions.
Can you fill them in?

1. The ———————— Man of Chelm.
2. The Wandering ————————.
3. "If my ———————— had ———————— she'd be a ————————."
4. Venerable Jewish curse: "May you grow like an ————————,
   with your feet in the air and your head in the ground."
5. "S. Hurok ————————."

Answers

Presents.
1. Wise. 2. Jew. 3. "If my *grandmother* had *wheels*, she'd be a *trol-
ley car*." (Or a slightly zestier version of your choice.) 4. Onion. 5.

＊

—— LAST NAMES ——

How long could Jews go on with "X son of Y" names? After centuries, they finally began to take surnames. Here's a matching
quiz of some last names and their meaning.

1. Rabinowitz	cobbler
2. Kaufman	wise
3. Schechter	rabbinical judge
4. Rothschild	merchant
5. Dayan	pearl
6. Cohen	tailor
7. Schneider	son of a rabbi
8. Schuster	red shield
9. Margolis	descended from a temple priest
10. Meyer	butcher

Cobbler. 9. Pearl. 10. Wise.
Rabbinical judge. 6. Descended from a temple priest. 7. Tailor. 8.
5. Son of a rabbi. 2. Merchant. 3. Butcher. 4. Red shield. 5.

LETTERS,
—— WE GET LETTERS . . . ——

Here are eight sets of initials that stand for Jewish organizations and expressions. Your task—as if you couldn't guess—is to spell out what they represent. Then answer the two final questions on letters.

1. UJA: _____.
2. JDL: _____.
3. ADL: _____.
4. BBG: _____.
5. JAP: _____.
6. USY: _____.
7. YMHA: _____.
8. AK: _____.

9. With what initials do you associate the London-born Jew Samuel Gompers?
10. And who is D.D. of the ILGWU?

1. United Jewish Appeal. 2. Jewish Defense League. 3. Anti-Defamation League (of the B'nai B'rith). 4. B'nai B'rith Girls. 5. Jewish-American Princess. 6. United Synagogue Youth. 7. Young Men's Hebrew Association. 8. Alter Kocker (an impolite expression meaning crotchety old man). 9. AFL (American Federation of Labor, the union he headed for twenty years). 10. David Dubinsky, president of the International Ladies' Garment Workers' Union.

—— TEAMWORK ——

Here's a section on Jewish people (and a few Jewish things) that belong in twos, threes, fours, and fives. Can you get it together and score well?

1. Once upon a time there was a Jewish comedy team, Mike and Elaine. They split and went on to their own things. Name them.
2. Two of the sixties' most popular singers were once known as Tom and Jerry. They became famous, however, as Paul and Art—their real names. They, too, split. Who were they?
3. A pair of songwriting brothers, G.G. and I.G. Who?
4. Joe and Lew, one of the top twosomes of vaudeville. Do you know them?
5. Why is the team of Shadrach, Meshach, and Abednego famous?
6. Who were three brothers of Hollywood fame named Al, Jimmy, and Harry?
7. One of the most famous Jewish teams in the twentieth century included Leonard, Arthur, Julius, and sometimes Herbert. Who were they?
8. Here's a team of five brothers closely associated with a Jewish holiday: Judah, Jonathan, Simon, John, and Eleazar. Who were they?

115

9. If you put Jewish wits like Dorothy Parker, Edna Ferber, Franklin P. Adams, and George S. Kaufman at a table with non-Jewish wits like Robert Benchley and Alexander Woollcott, what would you have?

10. One of the most famous Jewish teams of all isn't made of people. It's three items: one round and hard, one flat and pinkish, one white and spreadable. You find it on Sundays, mostly. What is it?

Answers

1. Nichols and May. 2. Simon and Garfunkel. 3. George and Ira Gershwin. 4. Weber and Fields. 5. In the Bible, they were the three thrown into a fiery furnace by Nebuchadnezzar. 6. The Ritz Brothers. 7. The Marx Brothers: Chico, Harpo, Groucho, and sometimes Zeppo. (Fifth brother Milton, or Gummo, was never in the act.) 8. The Maccabees, sons of Mattathias, well known for their role in the revolt against the Syrians in the Chanukah story. 9. The Algonquin Round Table, the famous luncheon group of New York's literary set. 10. Bagels, lox, and cream cheese.

—— THE ANSWER PERSON ——

Didn't you always want to write a quiz book? Well, here's your chance. This is a backward quiz, with the answers given; it's up to you to supply the best questions that are appropriate.

1. Milchig, flayshig, and pareve.
2. The four sons in the Passover Haggadah.
3. Twelve tones.
4. A character created by Leo Rosten under the pen name of Leonard Q. Ross.
5. Abbie and Julius J.
6. Lira and agorah.

7. A canopy held over the bride and groom at a wedding.
8. It's the portion of the Prophets read in the synagogue after the Torah reading; the bar mitzvah boy usually reads it.
9. They're both silent letters.
10. Vashti.

—— MISHMASH ——

Just an end-of-book grab bag of questions about a lot of Jewish information.

1. If someone "calls you to the bimah," is that someone
    A. dressing you down for something you did wrong?
    B. inviting you to read the Torah?
    C. inviting you to a wedding?
    D. offering you charity?
    E. ordering you to leave the synagogue?
2. P'tcha. There's an intriguing word. What do you do to it?
3. Who was Stephen Samuel Wise?

4. Was Belle Baker a famous
    A. scientist?   C. Zionist?
    B. singer?   D. portrait painter?
                    E. tennis player?
5. Joseph Strauss was a Jewish bridge engineer *par excellence.* His finest feat was the design of "The Bridge That Couldn't Be Built." What bridge was that?
6. What's the name of the widely used Orthodox code of Jewish law, a sixteenth-century compendium?
7. No, Josef Goebbels was not Jewish. But he had a powerful effect on millions of Jews. So this question: what was his function in the Hitler government?
8. The Talmud is a collection of writings that includes a compilation of the Oral Law and commentaries on it. What are the names for these two groups? (Bonus: In what language is each written?)
9. When we speak of the Talmud, we usually mean the works completed in Babylonia around the sixth century: the Babylonian Talmud. What is the earlier, shorter, less known Talmud?
10. With what college was Nat Holman associated? How?
11. Ben, as in David Ben Gurion, means _____.
12. How many psalms are there?
13. Where do mandlen belong?
    A. on a sweet tray   C. in shul
    B. at the foot of a bed   D. in soup
                    E. in your medicine chest
14. Asked to explain the difference between a misfortune and a calamity, the high British official concocted an example concerning his favorite political target: "If Gladstone fell into the Thames, that would be a misfortune. If someone pulled him out, that would be a calamity." Name that wit.
15. What did Jerome Robbins do to *West Side Story* and *Fiddler on the Roof?*

16. Felafel is
    A. a garment worn by ultra-orthodox Jews.
    B. a curse in Aramaic.
    C. a dish of fried chick-peas popular in Israel.
    D. a small animal mentioned in the Bible.
17. Where did the women's group Hadassah get its name?
18. What's the source of this quotation? "If I forget thee, O Jerusalem, Let my right hand forget her cunning; Let my tongue cleave to the roof of my mouth. . . ."
19. What Jewish humorist created Dobie Gillis, of book and TV fame?
20. Name an Israeli statesman whose first name reads the same forward and backward.

Answers

1. B. inviting you to read the Torah. 2. Eat it. (It's jellied calves' feet.) 3. A leading reform rabbi and Zionist. 4. B. singer. 5. San Francisco's Golden Gate Bridge. 6. The Shulchan Aruch. 7. Minister of Propaganda. 8. The Mishna and the Gemara. (Bonus: the first is in Hebrew, the second mostly in Aramaic.) 9. The Jerusalem (or Palestinian) Talmud. 10. College of the City of New York; as basketball coach (until the fifties fixing scandal). 11. Son of. 12. There are 150. 13. D. in soup. (They're airy soup nuts.) 14. Benjamin Disraeli. 15. He choreographed them both. 16. C. A dish of fried chick-peas in Israel (and New York). 17. Hadassah is Hebrew for the Persian name Esther, she being the heroine of the Purim story. 18. Psalm 137. 19. Max Shulman. 20. Abba Eban.

119

── FOR MAVENS ONLY ──

So you think these quizzes have been too easy? You're such a
gantzer k'nocker you knew all the answers? Well, perhaps this
final quiz will cut you down a bit, chochem! It's a rare bird who
can score more than twenty.

1. What nation other than Israel held Judaism to be the state
   religion?
2. The Shema gained its status as an important prayer in large
   part because of a famous rabbi of eighteen hundred years
   ago. Who?
3. What's an Uzzi?
4. Name the first Jew elected to public office in America.
   (Hint: he was a South Carolina legislator.)
5. What early superstar of the Yiddish theater in America—
   capable of roles ranging from high tragedy to low comedy—
   was nicknamed Nesher Agodl (Great Eagle)?
6. What did antipope Anacletus II have to do with the Jews?
7. And what about Poppaea Sabina, wife of King Nero? What
   was her Jewish link?
8. What was Samuel Gompers' trade?
9. If someone calls you a lamed vovnik, should you be flattered
   or annoyed? Explain.
10. You probably know that Jewish martyr Captain Alfred
    Dreyfus was court-martialed in the French Army, convicted
    of treason, and imprisoned on Devil's Island. But do you
    know what the "evidence" was?
11. And you should know also that Robert Briscoe was Lord
    Mayor of Dublin, but can you name the Jew who was Mayor
    of Rome from 1907 to 1913?
12. Ararat—from the mountain said to be the resting place of
    Noah's ark—was the name of a planned nineteenth-century
    refuge for Jews, something of a Western version of the Prom-
    ised Land. Where was it to be?

13. Who was the British economist of Sephardic background who wrote one of the major works of the theory of capitalism?

14. What's the big difference in gravestone customs between Sephardic and Ashkenazic Jews?

15. What was the name for the smallest unit of Israeli currency prior to 1960?

16. Tell who wrote this: "From a feeble cosmopolite I had turned into a fanatical anti-semite."

17. And who wrote this? "I will insist that the Hebrews have done more to civilize men than any other nation."

18. Numismatists know the name Victor David Brenner. Do you?

19. What Jewish ballplayer replaced Rogers Hornsby as Giants second baseman in 1928? (He didn't last long.)

20. Who was *second* prime minister of Israel?

21. It was a New York Jew who first publicly proposed the idea of adopting Britain's successful Daylight Savings Time in the States. Today, we all live by his idea. Who can name him?

22. What's Naftali Hertz Imber's claim to fame?

23. In which hand is the lulav carried?

24. What were the first two names of Britain's non-Jewish Minister of Foreign Affairs who gave his name to the Balfour Declaration?

25. Hermann Levi, born a Jew, was a good friend and colleague of a famous nineteenth-century German noted for his dislike of Jews. Do you know who?

26. Name the little Jewish strong man from vaudeville who pulled a 32-ton truck, bit iron chains in half, and crushed steel bars like Superman. He billed himself as "The Mighty Atom."

27. Who created the Yiddish-newspaper character Yenta Telebende?

28. What does YIVO stand for?

29. In the 1930s, Sidney Franklin, a Jewish boy from Brooklyn, did something no other Jewish boy from Brooklyn ever did. What?

30. "May the children of the stock of Abraham who dwell in this land continue to merit and enjoy the goodwill of the other inhabitants, while everyone shall sit in safety under his own vine and fig tree and there shall be none to make him afraid." Who wrote it?

Answers

1. The kingdom of the Khazars, a nomadic Turkish tribe that settled in southern Russia. The Khazar king chose Judaism in the eighth century and the empire remained officially Jewish for more than two hundred years, although only a minority of the people went along with the king. 2. Rabbi Akiba, who uttered it as he was being tortured to death for refusing to give up the reading of the Torah. 3. An Israeli-made automatic rifle. 4. Francis Salvador, an English immigrant who took office in January 1775. 5. Jacob Adler. 6. He was known as "the Jewish Pope," because of his Jewish ancestry. 7. She sympathized with the Jews and may have even converted to Judaism. 8. He was a cigar maker. 9. Very flattered. Lamed vov stands for thirty-six—the minimum number of righteous on whose behalf God allows the world to continue. So you're being placed among the three dozen most saintly individuals on earth. 10. An intercepted handwritten document addressed to a German military attaché, promising secret documents; the letter was later proved forged. 11. Ernesto Nathan. 12. On Grand Island, near Buffalo, New York. 13. David Ricardo. 14. The Sephardim use only flat gravestones, the Ashkenazim use standing stones. 15. The P'rutah. 16. Adolf Hitler (in Mein Kampf). 17. John Adams. 18. He was the Russian-Jewish immigrant who designed the Lincoln-head penny. 19. Andy Cohen. 20. Moshe Sharett. 21. Marcus M. Marks (then president of the Borough of Manhattan, New York City). 22. He wrote the words to "Hatikvah," the Israeli national anthem. 23. The right. 24. Arthur James. 25. Richard Wagner. (Levi conducted for him.) 26. Joseph L. Greenstein. 27. The writer B. Kovner. 28. The Yiddish initials of Yiddisher Vissenshaftlicher Institut, the Institute for Jewish Research. 29. He went to Mexico and Spain and became a prominent and successful bullfighter. 30. George Washington (to the Jews of Newport, Rhode Island).

HAVE YOU HEARD
THIS ONE?

It is dark and rainy and late at night. The secret agent slips inside a dingy tenement and walks upstairs, halting at apartment 3-A. He knocks twice, waits, knocks twice again, waits, and knocks once. The door opens a crack and a sleepy little man's head appears.

"Bernstein?" asks the agent.

"Yeah, what do you want?"

"When the sun shines, the bluebirds sing in the trees."

"Huh?"

"When the sun shines, the bluebirds sing in the trees."

The little man opens the door another inch and pushes his head into the hall.

"Oy, listen," he says wearily. "_____
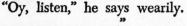_____."

"I'm Bernstein the *tailor.* You want Bernstein the spy. Upstairs in 4-A."

Zei Gezunt!